THE FOOD OF
CHINA

Authentic Recipes from the Middle Kingdom

Recipes by the chefs of Holiday Inn China
Food photography by Luca Invernizzi Tettoni
Introduction by Don J. Cohn
Editing by Wendy Hutton

PERIPLUS
EDITIONS

Distributed in the Continental United States by The Crossing Press

Contents

Part One: Food in China

ncient and superbly
nventive cuisine

: Marco
imagin-
entury.
the rich
r coun-

tributions to modern civilization, the most popular is Chinese food, enjoyed in restaurants and homes in every corner of the globe, from Iceland to Texas to Auckland. Few people in the world, with the possible exception of the French, are as passionately devoted to food as the Chinese. Meals are socially important events, and special menus are presented for weddings and birthdays; important festivals also have their traditional dishes and snacks.

What is the reason for the enduring worldwide popularity of Chinese food? It begins with a cornucopia of unique ingredients, vegetables and nourishing bean curd, plus subtle or emphatic sauces and seasonings that are partnered with just about every creature that swims the seas, flies the air or roams the land. This astonishing variety of ingredients is transformed by the Chinese into memorable works of culinary art. Every dish must meet three major criteria—appearance, fragrance and flavor; other considerations are texture, the health-giving properties of the food and its auspicious connotations.

The array of seasonings and sauces used by Chinese cooks is not vast; nor are a large range of culinary techniques employed. However, the endless interplay of one basic ingredient with another—meat with bean curd, vegetables with slivers of pork, lychees with shrimp, for example—and the transformation of these basics when combined with different seasonings, allows for almost endless variety.

Throughout its history, China has known a perpetual cycle of flood and famine. Food has always been a matter of desperate concern for its huge population (22 percent of the world's total, living on just 7 percent of the world's land). The paradox of Chinese food is that this cuisine, born of hardship and frequent poverty, is not one of dull subsistence but arguably the most creative in the world.

You can travel throughout China and the Chinese communities of Asia and never have the same dish served in exactly the same way twice. China's vast territory, diverse population and wide range of regional cuisines provide such infinite variety that eating in this ancient and inventive country is always an enjoyable adventure.

Page 2:
This charming naive painting by a folk artist living in a village west of Shanghai shows the entire family busy with preparation of stuffed dumplings.
***Opposite**:*
Three generations sit down to a meal in the courtyard of an old house in Fujian province, in Southern China.

Rice and Ritual

Six thousand years of culinary tradition

From the earliest times, the Chinese have divided their foodstuffs into two general categories: *fan* (cooked rice and staple grain dishes) and *cai* (cooked meat and vegetable dishes). This division dates back to the earliest recorded history, with bronze ritual vessels found in tombs from as early as the Zhou dynasty (1122–256 B.C.) designed to hold one or the other of these foodstuffs.

Grain includes the seeds of a wide range of plants. The earliest known grain appears to be millet, which was boiled or steamed. This was the staple of the early civilization in the north of China, probably as early as Neolithic times (7,000–5,000 B.C.), while by the Zhou dynasty, rice was the leading crop of the south. Wheat was also eaten in Neolithic China, but played a less prominent role than millet.

Archeology provides little clear evidence about the vegetables Neolithic Chinese cooked with their pork and dog meat, the earliest domesticated sources of animal protein. Beef, mutton and goat came later, although wild deer and rabbit probably appeared frequently on early menus. Fish and a variety of fowl were also used.

Early culinary techniques included boiling, steaming, roasting, stewing, pickling and drying. Stir-frying, the best known method today, probably developed later. In sum, it can be said that the basic Chinese diet and means of preparation were in place about 6,000 years ago, although many imported ingredients—some transported over the Silk Road—entered the Chinese larder and new cooking methods were adopted.

A balanced mixture of grain and cooked dishes has been the ideal of a meal in China since time immemorial. The balance lies between bland boiled or steamed grain on the one hand, and more flavorful and rich cooked dishes on the other. Further balances were sought between the *yin* (cooling) and *yang* (heating) qualities of the foods served. The notion of food as both preventative and curative medicine is deeply imbedded in the Chinese psyche.

The specific proportion of grain and cooked dishes on a menu depends as much on the economic status of the diners as on the status of the occasion. Traditionally, grain would provide the bulk of the calories, with cooked dishes serving as supplementary ornamentation and nutrition. The grander the occasion, the more cooked dishes and less grain. Even today, this tradition is maintained at banquets, where a small symbolic bowl of plain steamed rice is served after an extensive selection of other dishes.

Rice is perceived as something essential and almost magical. This is particularly true in South

China, while wheat showers its blessings over the North, although this division is not hard and fast. One reason the Grand Canal was built in the 6th century was to transport rice from the fertile Yangtze delta region to the imperial granaries in the relatively dry North. And since the Ming dynasty (1368–1644), an annual crop of short-grain rice has been grown in the suburbs of Beijing, originally for the palace and today for the military leadership.

Numerous varieties of rice are produced in China today, supplemented by more expensive Thai rice, which is available at urban markets throughout the country. Southerners seem to prefer long-grained rice, which is less sticky than other varieties and has strong "wood" overtones when steaming hot.

Rice is served steamed, fried (after boiling) or made into noodles by grinding raw rice into rice flour. It is also cooked with a lot of water to produce congee or *zhou* (rice gruel), a popular breakfast food and late-night snack eaten with a number of savory side dishes.

In early times, wheat was boiled like rice, but by the Han dynasty (220 B.C.–A.D. 200), the grain was ground into flour and made into noodles, pancakes and various forms of dumplings, some of the recipes having possibly been imported from Cen-

An old Chinese painting depicting an obviously important and wealthy Chinese gentleman being entertained by a woman playing music while being tempted with a range of delicacies.

tral Asia. It is unlikely that Marco Polo brought spaghetti, linguine and pizza to Italy from China. Although their prototypes existed in China centuries before he was born, there is written evidence of the existence of pasta in Italy before the Polos left home for the East.

A noted connoisseur of French food complained some forty years ago that all Chinese food tastes "half cooked." Today, food that is half raw or half cooked (the terminology is subjective and interchangeable) seems to be more acceptable, even fashionable, inspired by considerations of health. But who needs the pursuit of longevity as an excuse to enjoy Chinese food?

North, South, East and West

China's regional cuisines: not so much a matter of what you eat but how you cook it

It was not so long ago that everyone in the West thought of "Chinese food" as a single cuisine. A country as large and as geographically and climatically varied as China naturally has a wide range of regional cuisines. There is an immense amount of debate, confusion and error about just how many regional cuisines there are, but most knowledgeable gourmets agree that at least four major Chinese regional styles exist: Cantonese, centered on southern Guangdong province and Hong Kong; Sichuan, based on the cooking of this western province's two largest cities, Chengdu and Chongqing; Huaiyang, the cooking of eastern China—Jiangsu, Zhejiang and Shanghai—an area of lakes, rivers and seashore; and Beijing or "Northern" food, with its major inspiration from the coastal province of Shandong. Some would add a fifth cuisine from the southeastern coastal province of Fujian.

What distinguishes these regional styles is not only their recipes but also the particular types of soy sauce, garlic, fish, oil, pork or other basic ingredients used in preparing the signature dishes, as well as the proportions of the various ingredients. Timing and temperature are also critical factors. All regions use various forms of ginger, garlic, spring onions, soy sauce, vinegar, sugar, sesame oil and bean paste, but generally combine them in highly distinctive ways.

Guangdong province has benefitted from its family ties with freewheeling Hong Kong. The province's fertile soils permit intensive agricultural production and its lengthy shoreline supports a vigorous fishing industry. In a longstanding rivalry with Shanghai, Guangzhou (the provincial capital, once better known to Westerners as Canton) cedes first place in fashion, but is the unchallenged leader when it comes to food.

The earliest Chinese cuisine to be introduced in the West, Cantonese cuisine is often disparagingly identified with egg rolls, chop suey, chow mein, sweet and sour pork and fortune cookies. With the exception of chop suey and fortune cookies, which were invented in the United States, the dishes men-

tioned above are orthodox Cantonese creations, and Sweet and Sour Pork is just as popular among Chinese as foreigners. But Cantonese cooking has much more to offer than this, and indeed is considered to be the most refined of Chinese cooking styles. Cantonese food is characterized by its extraordinary range and freshness of ingredients, a light touch with sauces and the readiness of its cooks to incorporate "exotic" imported flavorings, such as lemon, curry, Worcestershire sauce and mayonnaise.

Cantonese chefs excel in preparing roast and barbecued meats (duck, goose, chicken and pork), which are never prepared at home (only restaurant kitchens have ovens) and are bought from special roast meat shops.

Cantonese chefs are also famous for *dim sum*, a cooking style in its own right. *Dim sum* refers to snacks taken with tea for either breakfast or lunch. *Dim sum* can be sweet, salty, steamed, fried, baked, boiled or stewed, small dishes each served in their own individual bamboo steamer or plate.

In Cantonese, eating *dim sum* is referred to as *yum cha,* "drinking tea." In traditional *yum cha* establishments, restaurant staff walk about the room pushing a cart or carrying a tray strung around their neck and offer their goods. The mildly competitive

A cheerful waitress pushes a cart filled with some of the baked and deep-fried tidbits that are part of the popular Cantonese array of dim sum.

shouting only adds to the atmosphere of hustle and bustle. In Hong Kong and Guangzhou, *dim sum* restaurants are important institutions where the locals go to discuss business, read newspapers, raise their children and socialize. At noon and on weekends, getting seats can be difficult as many of them are occupied by "regulars."

The home of spicy food and of Chinese leader Deng Xiaoping, Sichuan is a landlocked province with remarkably fertile soil and a population of more than 100 million. But despite the province's incendiary reputation, many of the most famous dishes are not spicy at all. For example, the famous duck dish, Camphor and Tea Smoked Duck, is made by smoking a steamed duck over a mixture of tea and camphor leaves.

But it is the mouth-burners (all of them relying on chili peppers for their heat) that have made Sichuan's name known all over the world, dishes like Ma Po Dou Fu, stewed bean curd and minced meat in a hot sauce; Hui Guo Rou, twice-cooked (boiled and stir fried) pork with cabbage in a piquant bean sauce; Yu Xiang Qiezi, eggplant in "fish flavor" sauce and Dou Ban Yu, fish in hot bean sauce.

Chilies were a relatively late addition to the Sichuan palate, having been imported by Spanish traders in the late Ming or early Qing dynasty (ca. 1600) from Mexico via the Philippines. The chili's journey on the Pacific Spice Route is a reminder of how plants, as well as ideas, can cross oceans and enrich the lives of the recipients. Sichuan's own taste-tingling spice, Sichuan pepper (fagara or prickly ash) still adds its distinctive flavor to many of the province's dishes.

The taste for piquant food is sometimes explained by Sichuan's climate. The fertile agricultural basin is covered with clouds much of the year and there is enough rain to permit two crops of rice in many places. Strong spices provide a pick-me-up in cold and humid weather and are a useful preservative for meat and fish.

When the Grand Canal was built in the Sui dynasty (A.D. 581–618), it gave rise to several great commercial cities at its southern terminus, including Huaian and Yangzhou, after which this regional cuisine (Huaiyang) is named. The region's location on the lower reaches of the Yangtze River in China's "land of fish and rice" (synonymous with the Western "milk and honey") gave it a distinct advantage in terms of agricultural products, and it was renowned for such aquatic delicacies as fish, shrimp, eel and crab, which were shipped up the canal to the imperial court in Beijing. The cooking of Jiangsu, Zhejiang and Shanghai generally falls into the category of Huaiyang cuisine, which was developed by the great families of the imperially appointed salt merchants living in Yangzhou.

Huaiyang cuisine is not well known outside of China, perhaps because it rejects all extremes and strives for the "Middle Way." Freshness (*xian*) is a key concept in the food of this region, but *xian* means more than just fresh. For example, for a dish of steamed fish to be *xian,* the fish must have been swimming in the tank one hour ago, it must exude its own natural flavor, and must be tender yet slightly chewy.

Xian also implies that the natural flavor of the original ingredients should take precedence over the sauce, and Huaiyang chefs achieve this by careful cutting and paying close attention to the heat of wok, which is, after all, merely a thin and sensitive membrane of cast iron separating the ingredients from the flames of the stove. Chinese chefs, and Huaiyang chefs in particular, control the flames of their stoves like a pianist uses the pedal.

Some of the best-known Huaiyang dishes are steamed or stewed and thus require less heat and a longer cooking time than most fried dishes; examples include Chicken with Chestnuts, Pork Steamed in Lotus Leaves, Duck with an Eight-In-

Steamed dumplings are popular in most regions of China, and connoisseurs can recognize their provincial origin by their stuffing and accompanying sauces.

gredient Stuffing, and "Lion Head" Meatballs.

The cuisine of Beijing has perhaps been subjected to more outside influences than any other major cuisine in China. First came the once-nomadic Mongols, who made Beijing their capital in the Yuan dynasty (1279–1368). They brought with them a preference for mutton, the chief ingredient in Mutton or Mongolian Hot Pot, one of Beijing's most popular dishes in the autumn and winter.

And then there were the Manchus, who, as the rulers of the Qing dynasty (1644–1911), introduced numerous ways of cooking pork. As the capital of China for the last eight centuries, Beijing became the home of government officials who brought their chefs with them when they came from the wealthy southern provinces of Jiangsu and Zhejiang. But the most important influence comes from nearby Shandong province; in the 19th century, the restaurant industry in Beijing was monopolized by entrepreneurs from Shandong.

Shandong food has a pedigree that goes back to the days of Confucius (ca. 550 B.C.), who was a Shandong native. Shandong cuisine features the seafood found along China's eastern seaboard: scallops and squid, both dry and fresh, sea cucumber, conch, crabs, bird's nests and shark's fins. Shandong cuisine is also famous for its use of spring onions and leeks, both raw and cooked.

Beijing's most famous dish, Beijing Roast Duck, owes as much to the culinary traditions of other parts of China as to the capital itself. The ducks themselves, now raised in the western suburbs of Beijing, are said to have swum up the Grand Canal in the wake of imperial grain barges, dining on rice that blew off the boats. The method of roasting the duck is drawn from Huaiyang cuisine, while the pancakes, raw leek and salty sauce that accompany the meat are typical of Shandong.

Beijing is also famous for its steamed and boiled dumplings (*jiaozi*), which are filled with a mixture of pork and cabbage or leeks, or a combination of eggs and vegetables. Dipped in vinegar and soy sauce and accompanied with a nibble of raw garlic, they are one of the simplest but finest pleasures of Chinese cuisine.

Regional cuisine is so popular in China today that in Beijing and Shanghai, for example, there are many more restaurants serving Cantonese and Sichuan food—or advertising that they do—than there are establishments serving local cuisine. Western fast food restaurants have made an impact, but more as a novelty than a staple of the diet. Chinese food, in all its glory, is here to stay.

Opposite:
One of China's most famous regional dishes, Peking Duck is traditionally enjoyed three ways: the crisp skin tucked into a pancake smeared with sauce; the meat stir fried with vegetables and the carcass made into soup.
Left:
The roasting of chicken, duck and pork is done in wood-fired ovens in specialty shops and restaurants, as home kitchens lack an oven.

Home and Market

From daily marketing to street stalls, food is all important for China's millions

The proliferation of refrigerators in China today is making inroads on an institution that for centuries has been an essential part of daily life: shopping in the local food market. Quite unwittingly, markets in China make excellent destinations for tourists, sociologists and economists. Here one can observe the locals squeezing fruits—and fruit sellers squeezing the customers— and the high-pitched haggling that revolves around the price of a fistful of pork in which less than a penny, but lots of face, is at stake. You may also observe how the emerging middle class and *nouveaux riches* interact with the food sellers, who are usually of peasant origin. There was greater civility in China ten years ago before the emergence of this new "class."

Nutritious and versatile bean curd, one of the many products bought daily by the Chinese housewife, comes in a variety of forms.

Most dealers have their regular customers and try to please them by throwing in the extra strawberry or potato or backing off on the price now and then. With six people selling exactly the same cucumbers, tomatoes and string beans within earshot, competition is fierce.

Many men and women go to the market two or three times a day. In some state-run offices in Beijing, for example, half-hour rest periods are allotted for shopping for lunch and dinner. Although prices are not marked on most stands, the average housewife knows the price of every item in the market and what she paid for half a pound of taro two weeks ago. Food in China may appear inexpensive compared to the West, but food purchases consume 40–60 percent of the average household budget, as rent for many is negligible.

In addition to fresh food markets, there are shops selling a huge variety of prepared and packaged food, which can be fascinating for the first-time visitor. China's open policy since 1978 has resulted in "100 flowers blooming" in the area of comestibles, particularly in the major cities, where people have more disposable time and cash than ever before and seem willing to dabble in new taste sensations. In addition to Western and Chinese fast foods, there are excellent bakeries, many of them joint ventures, and a range of "natural" health food products of remarkable sophistication.

Along with food markets, most cities have areas where snack foods are sold in stand-up or sit-down stalls. Breakfast is well catered for in almost every city, as the morning meal is the one people are most likely to eat outside the home or work place. Popular breakfasts are a fried egg wrapped in a pancake; an "elephant ear" plate-size piece of fried bread; noodles; congee (rice gruel) or bean curd jelly accompanied by a deep-fried cruller (*you tiao*) or a slice of cake and a jar of milk.

Every region has its own particular snacks, very often sold on the street. Snack food is very inexpensive and includes such regional specialties as Beijing's boiled tripe with fresh coriander, fried starch sausage with garlic, sour bean soup, and boiled pork and leek dumplings (*jiaozi*). Shanghai is known for its steamed *baozi* dumplings, sweet glutinous rice with eight sweetmeats (*babaofan*) and yeasty sweetened wine lees. Sichuan is noted for spicy *dan dan* noodles, dumplings in hot sauce and bean curd jelly (*dou hua*), while Cantonese *dim sum* is a cuisine unto itself.

The average urban family eats its main meal of the day in the evening. This meal usually consists of a staple such as rice or noodles, one or two fried dishes, at least one of which contains meat or fish, and a soup. Beer regularly accompanies meals at home; stronger spirits are reserved for special occasions. Cramped quarters make it difficult for home cooking to be fancy, but Sunday provides a good excuse for moderate culinary excesses. The whole family gets involved in the business of shop-

Inexpensive and generally delicious street food, such as these dumplings being fried in a Shanghai lane, is enjoyed at least once a day by most Chinese living in towns and cities.

ping and cooking, and friends or relatives may be invited to join in the feast.

Western foods have made tentative sallies into the 6,000-year-old bastion of Chinese cuisine, but fast food outlets succeed mainly because of their novelty and location. Western fast food can only be sustained in Chinese tourist cities. For the vast bulk of the population, it's rice and vegetables like Mother used to make, not Colonel Sanders' secret recipe.

All the Tea in China

Tea is the all-important drink, although wine has a much longer tradition

Tea is a critical ingredient in Chinese life. Tea is drunk before a meal and after a meal, but rarely during a meal. Tea is drunk all day at work, at rest, when alone or with friends. Indeed, it is hard to imagine a situation in which tea is not present. Tea drinking is a Chinese invention, although the plant may have first been grown in Southeast Asia. In any case, the written record suggests that tea has been cultivated and drunk in China since the Han dynasty (220 B.C.–A.D. 200).

Tea is more than just a drink in China, and the teahouse, where men gather to gossip, occupies much the same social role as a pub in England or a bar in France.

The Japanese tea ceremony, which makes use of powdered tea and a bamboo brush to beat the tea until a froth appears on the surface, was inspired by Chinese tea customs in the Tang dynasty. But the custom of drinking steeped leaf tea, as we know it today, began only during the Ming dynasty (1368–1644). This accompanied the emergence of fine white porcelain that showed off the color and shape of the leaves to their best advantage.

There is only one tea plant, but many types of tea. Variations in color and flavor are obtained by the time of picking, fermentation, rolling and roasting. Generally speaking, there are three types of tea: unfermented green tea, such as Longjing (Dragon Well); semi-fermented tea, such as Oolong and fermented tea, such as the "black tea" (in Chinese, it is called "red tea") most popular in India and the West. Green tea is further mixed with jasmine blossoms to make jasmine tea, a favorite summer drink in North China. In South China, from Guangdong west to Yunnan, musty-rusty Pu'er tea is the most common drink.

Tea can be steeped in a pot or a cup. Fastidious drinkers will discard the first, brief steeping as a way of cleaning the leaves and dilating them for the second steeping, regarded by many as the best. Good tea can be steeped as many as ten times.

Judging from wine vessels found in archeological sites, it is likely that wine was first made in China from grain using the method of yeast fermentation around 5,000 years ago, when it was offered to the god of the sun and the ancestors in rituals.

Grapes and grape wine were introduced to China from the West around 150 B.C., and the technique of distilling wine from *kaoliang*, a form of sorghum, became popular around the Song dynasty, some 800 years ago. The great Tang poet Li Bai (Li Po), who gained a reputation as a drinker, most likely drew his inspiration from fermented rice wine. Today, grape wine is again being produced in the Western fashion and there are a number of successful joint-venture wineries producing Chardonnay, Riesling, "Champagne" and varieties of red wine.

The leading Chinese-style grain wines are classified as either "white" (*bai jiu*) or "yellow" (*huang jiu*). White wines are distilled spirits with an alcohol content ranging from 40 to 60 percent. The most famous brand of white—more accurately clear—spirits is Maotai, made in the southwest province of Guizhou. These potent drinks are usually taken "straight up" in small cups or glasses during a meal.

Yellow wine, distilled from glutinous rice, is produced in the coastal area near Shanghai. The most famous source is Shaoxing, in Zhejiang province. Yellow wine has an alcohol content of approximately 14 percent and is often compared to dry sherry. It is frequently used in cooking and imparts a rich, yeasty flavor to fish and many other dishes.

The history of beer brewing in China goes back more than a century to the German concession in Qingdao (or Tsingtao), on the coast of Shandong province. Qingdao is still home to the largest brewery in China today, and there are dozens of regional breweries. Believe it or not, three billion beer bottles circulate freely among the breweries in China, and a bottle of beer costs no more than 25 cents.

Since 1990, food markets in China have been flooded with bottled mineral water; at present there are over 1,000 "sources" throughout the country. Several companies have also started selling distilled and filtered drinking water, yet another sign of the rising standard of living in China. Chinese (understandably) never drink unboiled tap water. The strong chlorine taste in most city water—particularly in the Shanghai area where much of the drinking water is taken from the Yangtze and has a muddy fragrance as well—makes these bottled waters a welcome change, particularly for making tea, soup, rice and noodles.

A surprising range of wines and spirits is found in special wine shops in China's towns and cities. Cooking wine made from glutinous rice is also found in regular provision shops.

China's Gourmet Culture

The paradox of conspicuous consumption in a socialist society

Archeological evidence in the form of stone carvings in early tombs suggests that the emperors and the aristocracy in ancient China ate well in terms of quantity. But did the contents of their great bronze cauldrons actually taste good?

We will never know the answer to this question, but we can assume that the emperors had at their disposal the best and widest variety of ingredients in the land, as well as the best chefs. We do know from historical records that in the Song dynasty, some of the best aristocratic houses had kitchen staffs of more than 100 people, and would also send out for special dishes prepared in local restaurants. Thus the idea of "take out" or "carry away" Chinese restaurants goes back a long way in history.

Annals of the Tang dynasty capital at Chang'an (present day Xi'an), arguably the greatest city in the world in the 8th and 9th centuries, reveal that there were many Indian and Central Asian restaurants and others selling food from the western end of the Silk Road, as well as wine shops where the hostesses had light hair and blue eyes.

Numerous historical figures were known for their capacity for food and drink, but China's best known gourmet is Yuan Mei, who lived in the 18th century. Yuan left a wonderful book of recipes and miscellaneous jottings on eating (*Suiyuan shidan*), re-vealing himself as both a fine chef and great aesthete. Yuan wrote specifically about which foods combined well and which did not—crab roe should not be cooked with bird's nest, for example—and commented about the excesses of the day. He was once invited to a banquet at the home of a governor who served each guest a huge pot full of unflavored bird's nest. Yuan Mei remarked: "We are here to eat swallow's nest, not to take delivery of it wholesale."

Such conspicuous consumption would not be entirely out of place in China today, as economic liberalization and the resulting upward mobility have spawned thousands of restaurants in the towns and cities. For example, in 1948, Beijing had some 3,000 restaurants catering to every class of society, from rickshaw pullers to bankers. By 1953, following the revolution and closing of private businesses, there were only 300 restaurants left in the city, most of them unimaginatively named "The People's Restaurant" or "The Masses Dining Hall." The proletarian philistinism of the Cultural Revolution (1966–76) had a disastrous effect on China's finer restaurants and chefs, many of whom never cooked again.

But after 1978, the number of restaurants (vegetarian included) mushroomed and today there are at least 3,000 restaurants, large and small, in the capital, once again catering to a wide range of pocket-

Opposite: Esoteric and often extremely expensive ingredients such as dried shark's fin, dried scallops and dried oysters go into some of China's most prized dishes. The dried lizard (bottom right) is reserved for medicinal soups.

Banquets are important social and commercial events in China today and many high officials attend banquets five or six nights a week. Almost any event can supply the reason for a banquet: the completion (or non-completion) of a business deal, wedding, graduation, trip abroad, return from a trip abroad, promotion, moving house and so on. One can also give a banquet to save or give "face" in the case of some unpleasant situation or mishap.

Some of the best restaurants in China today are the pre-1949 enterprises that have managed to survive by virtue of the quality of their cooking and by their location. One example is Fangshan Restaurant in Beihai Park in Beijing, set in a former imperial palace on the shores of a man-made lake, where many of the recipes are taken from the late Qing dynasty Forbidden City. Fangshan is renowned for its Manchu-Chinese Banquet, a three-day dining extravaganza that consists of more than 100 different dishes in all, a souvenir of Qing-dynasty court banquets. At another famous restaurant, Listening to the Orioles Pavilion, in the gardens of the famed Summer Palace (known to the Chinese as Yi He Yuan), dinners for 10 at around $1,000 per table are reputedly not uncommon.

China's gourmet culture has it roots in the imperial palace and filtered down to the private homes of the rich and powerful and to the restaurants where the privileged entertained. To some extent, this economic model persists today, although Chinese culture—including education, values, taste, consumption patterns—in the 1990s is separated from the still-traditional culture of the 1920s and 1930s by much more than just a few decades.

books. Joint-venture restaurants offer authentic Hong Kong-style Cantonese food, and most hotels have a Sichuan restaurant in addition to a French or Italian and a Japanese outlet. As in the old days, some restaurants survive by charging the highest possible prices; you can identify them by the number of Mercedes, Cadillacs, Lincolns and BMWs parked outside, as well as by the shark's fins, bird's nests and lobsters on the menu.

The Emperor's Banquet

One hundred dishes per meal yet not one dining room in sight

As the Son of Heaven, the emperor of China enjoyed a status so elevated above the common mortal that it is difficult to conceive of the awe in which he was held and the power that he enjoyed. In the realm of food, however, the emperor was subject to numerous restrictions.

The emperor could, however, take his meals at any time and in any place. In fact, there are no dining rooms *per se* in the Forbidden City; tables would be set up before the emperor wherever he decided to eat.

Every meal was a banquet of approximately 100 dishes. These included 60 or 70 dishes from the imperial kitchens, and a few dozen more served by the chief concubines from their own kitchens. For reasons of security, however, the emperor could not order a specific dish lest it be poisoned the next time it was served. Nor could he express a positive opinion about any particular dish. Security was monitored by inserting a silver rod into each dish, which would turn black if it came into contact with arsenic. At every meal the emperor dined off mu-

The last Dowager Empress of China may well have dined in this very spot, on the edge of the lake in the gardens of the Summer Palace outside Beijing.

seum-quality porcelain, with gold, silver, jade, rhinoceros horn, lacquer tableware and chopsticks.

Many of the dishes were made purely for their visual appeal and were placed far away from the reach of the imperial chopsticks. These leftovers were spirited out of the palace to be sold to gourmets eager to "dine with the emperor."

Fastidious records were kept in the imperial kitchen, which had more than 100 woks, with three men assigned to each. The names of each dish made by the chefs and the amount of ingredients used were recorded. At one imperial banquet held on the eve of Chinese New Year in 1784, the emperor Qianlong was personally served a total of about 300 pounds of meat, including three ducks, ten chickens, six pheasants, five geese, 264 pounds of boar, 22 pounds of mutton, 22 pounds of fish and four deer's tails.

Today, Fangshan and Listening to the Orioles Pavilion, two restaurants in Beijing, specialize in dishes said to be prepared according to the authentic imperial recipes.

Don't Point with Your Chopsticks

A few basic rules for wining and dining in Chinese society

Don't point with your chopsticks and don't stick your chopsticks into your rice bowl and leave them there standing up, for in this position they resemble incense sticks set before a grave.

Don't use your chopsticks to explore the contents of a dish. Locate the morsel you want—on top of the pile, not buried in the middle of it—with your eyes and go directly for it with your chopsticks without touching any other pieces. A wait-and-see-attitude is recommended if you wish to land the white meat, the wing or the chicken heart.

If you wish to take a drink of wine at a formal dinner, you must first toast

another diner, regardless of whether he or she responds by drinking. If you are toasted and don't wish to drink, simply touch your lips to the edge of the wine glass to acknowledge the courtesy.

It is incumbent upon the host to urge the guests to eat and drink to their fill. This means ordering more food than necessary and keeping an eye out for idle chopsticks. It is polite to serve the guest of honor the best morsels, such as the cheek of the fish,

using a pair of serving or "public" chopsticks or with the back end of one's chopsticks.

If you have had enough to eat, yet your host still plies you with food, or if you do not wish to indulge in fish lips, sea cucumber or duck web, graciously allow your host to place the delicacy on your plate; leaving food uneaten indicates you do not care for it.

It is socially acceptable in China to spit bones on the table, belch, slurp soup and noodles and smoke while eating.

Rice can be eaten by raising the bowl to the mouth and shoveling the grains in with the chopsticks in a rapid fanning motion, even though this may resemble a Beijing duck force feeding itself.

Chinese banquets commonly have 12–20 courses in succession and can last for hours, but the dinner is over when the host stands up and offers the final toast; one is expected to leave immediately thereafter. Chatting at the table over coffee after a meal or retiring to the drawing room is not part of Chinese etiquette.

This child seems more concerned with eating than etiquette, but will no doubt pick up the finer points of dining as he grows up.

Part Two: The Chinese Kitchen

*A combination of simple utensils and
techniques perfected over the centuries*

Perhaps the most surprising aspect of a Chinese kitchen is its utter simplicity. It's hard to believe that such creative and often sophisticated food is prepared with so few utensils. Even today, most cooks manage with a coal-fired stove, basically a bench top with several holes of differing sizes where woks, clay pots and saucepans are placed.

The most essential ingredient is a **wok**, a parabolic pan traditionally made of cast iron and used for just about everything except cooking rice: stir frying, deep frying, braising, making sauces, holding a steaming basket and so on. The shape of the wok distributes the heat evenly, while its sloping sides ensure that during stir frying, food falls back into the pan and not out over the edge. It's also practical for deep frying, requiring less oil than a conventional saucepan or frying pan.

A wok should be "seasoned" before its first use so that food will not stick to it. Wash the inside of the wok with warm soapy water but do not use a scouring pad. Rinse with fresh water and dry thoroughly. Put some oil on a piece of paper towel and wipe the inside of the wok. Repeat two or three times until the paper towel stays clean after wiping. Store the wok until ready to use it. Chinese cooks always heat the wok before adding oil to be sure that it is dry and the oil will not splatter. After cooking, never clean your wok with detergent or harsh abrasives; just rinse it with warm water and wipe dry.

Clay pots of various shapes and sizes, with a sandy outside and a glazed interior, are used for slow cooking and for making soups and stocks. These are attractive and inexpensive, but any type of saucepan could be used instead. Rice is usually cooked in an aluminum or stainless steel **saucepan**, although more and more affluent homes in the cities boast an electric rice cooker.

Just as indispensable as the wok is a **cleaver**, which comes with either a heavy rectangular blade about 3–4 inches deep, ideal for cutting through bones, or a lighter weight blade for chopping, slicing, bruising garlic cloves and scooping up food on the flat edge to carry it to the pan. One single Chinese cleaver does the work of a whole battery of knives in a Western kitchen.

Partner to the cleaver is a strong **chopping board**, in China, a thick cross section of a tree trunk.

Meat is always minced on a board, using a couple of cleavers; a food processor achieves a similar result with much less effort and skill required.

Steaming is a healthy method of cooking favored by the Chinese, who traditionally use a multi-tiered bamboo **steamer** with a woven cover that absorbs any moisture, unlike a metal cover where moisture condenses and falls down on the food. The steaming basket is placed inside a wok, sitting a few inches above the boiling water. Chinese stores also sell perforated metal disks that sit inside a wok above the water level; these are useful for steaming a single plate of food. For steaming in this fashion, you will need to buy a large, dome-shaped lid that will cover your wok.

Other useful utensils include a **wire mesh basket** on a long handle, good for scooping out deep-fried food or boiled noodles. A round-edged **frying spatula** is perfect for tossing stir-fried ingredients in the wok. Chinese cooks also like a pair of **long wooden chopsticks** for turning over food during deep frying, though this does require a certain dexterity and you may be happier with tongs.

Cooking methods include steaming, stir frying, braising, deep frying and slow cooking. Roasted food is always bought from a specialty shop as home kitchens lack an oven.

Stir frying is by far the most commonly used method. Oil is heated in the wok and evenly sliced ingredients tossed about constantly; contact with the heat from the sides as well as the bottom of the wok means that food cooks very rapidly, sealing in the juices and flavor.

Timing is absolutely crucial to the success of Chinese dishes. Most food is cooked very briefly (a result of centuries of having to conserve precious fuel), so it is essential to chop all ingredients, measure all the seasonings, and have the garnishes and serving dishes at hand before starting to cook.

Control of heat is also important, and for this reason, a gas flame is far superior to any other form of heat. The degree of heat required for some dishes, especially for stir frying, is far greater than that normally used in a Western kitchen.

Timing given in the recipes in this book assumes that very high heat can be used when called for; if you doubt the intensity of your source of heat, try cooking the food for just a little longer. If you have an electric stove, you might consider investing in a single gas burner capable of producing extremely high heat and of immediate temperature control, otherwise your results will not be the same.

One single wok can be used to cook the entire meal, except for the rice. The first dish is cooked, the wok quickly rinsed with water, dried and the next batch of ingredients put in. Naturally, the Chinese cook doesn't have to break off in the middle of cooking to check the recipe. Make sure you prepare and place ingredients near your stove in order of use so you can work as quickly as possible, and have your serving plates ready. And remember, as any Chinese cook would agree, practice makes perfect.

*A bamboo steamer (**above**) and long-handled scoops (**below left**) are some of the basic utensils found in any Chinese kitchen; the oil pot (**below right**) for drizzling oil into the wok is an attractive option.*

Chinese Ingredients

Increasingly available around the world, authentic ingredients give the true taste of China

BAMBOO SHOOTS: Fresh bamboo shoots must be peeled, sliced and simmered in water for about 30 minutes. Boil canned bamboo shoots for 5 minutes to reduce any metallic flavor before using.

BEAN CURD: Several types of bean curd are made from the coagulated "milk" extracted from soy beans. Squares of thick **soft bean curd** (*dou hua*) are used mainly for soups and stir-fried dishes where the "scrambling" of the bean curd is a characteristic of the dish. Bean curd is compressed to make **hard bean curd** (*dou fu*). Squares of brownish **dried, deep-fried bean curd** are crisp on the outside and porous within; blanch briefly with boiling water to remove excess oil before using. Sheets of dried **bean curd skin**, made from the skin that forms on boiling soy bean milk, are used as a wrapping, while long strips of dried bean curd skin are sometimes added to meat or vegetable dishes. Small squares of either red or white **fermented bean curd**, sold in jars, are used to flavor some Chinese dishes.

BEAN SPROUTS: Sprouted green mung peas are more commonly used than soy bean sprouts both in China and abroad. Store in a refrigerator covered with water for 2–3 days, changing water daily. The straggly tails can be pinched off just before use, if desired.

BLACK BEANS, SALTED: Fermented salted black beans are used to season a number of dishes, especially fish and beef. Sold in packets or cans, they can be kept several months if stored in a covered jar in the refrigerator. Rinse before use to remove excess salt.

BLACK MOSS FUNGUS: A fine, hair-like fungus (*fa cai*, or *fatt choy* in Cantonese) which should be soaked in warm water until swollen.

BOX THORN BERRIES: Oval red berries, sometimes known as wolf berries, prized for their medicinal properties. Available in Chinese medicine shops.

CATERPILLAR FUNGUS: Neither a caterpillar nor a fungus, these dried pods (*Cordyceps sinensis*) are used in some dishes for their medicinal value.

CENTURY EGG: Also known by several different names, including 100-year eggs and 1000-year eggs. Duck eggs are coated with a mixture of powdered lime, rice husks and salt and left

Bamboo Shoots

Salted Black Beans

Black Moss Fungus

Box Thorn Berries

Caterpillar Fungus

Cinnamon

Cloud Ear Fungus

to cure for several months. Peel off the shell, then quarter or chop the eggs, which have a translucent black albumen and greenish yolk.

CHICKEN STOCK POWDER: Loose granules of chicken stock are used to add extra flavor to certain dishes, especially by creative Cantonese chefs. As this powder is often quite salty, taste the dish before adding any salt. Substitute instant chicken broth mix or instant chicken bouillon powder.

CHILI: Finger-length **red chilies**, both fresh and dried, are more commonly used than unripe **green chilies**. **Chili paste**, sold in jars, varies from one region to another in China, and often contains additional ingredients. A Chinese brand is preferable, although any Southeast Asian chili paste could be substituted. **Sichuan chili paste** is made from dried chilies, soaked and ground with a touch of oil. **Chili sauce** is similar in texture to tomato sauce (ketchup) and is sold in bottles. **Chili oil**, which can be bought or made, is used to enliven some Sichuan dishes.

CHINESE CABBAGE: The three most commonly used types are: ***bok choy*** (*bai cai*), which has white stems and bright green leaves and is often sold in immature form (see garnish for Braised Pork Leg, page 117); **Napa** or **"celery" cabbage**, which has long pale green leaves and white celery-like stems and **round green cabbage**, the type most commonly found in the West.

CHINESE WINE: Various types of Chinese "yellow" wine made from fermented rice are used in cooking. Wine made in Shaoxing is generally considered the best and should be available in any Chinese food store; dry sherry could be used as a substitute.

CHIVES: "Chinese" or "coarse" chives, dark green flat leaves about 12 inches long, are used as a vegetable and seasoning. Their flavor is stronger than normal chives, which is why they are sometimes known as "garlic" chives. Sometimes sold with flowering heads.

CILANTRO: Fresh coriander leaf, sometimes known as "Chinese parsley," is used as a garnish or in some stuffings. It has a distinctive fragrance totally unlike regular parsley.

CINNAMON: The bark of the cassia tree, thicker and stronger in flavor than true cinnamon, is used in some Chinese dishes.

CLOUD EAR FUNGUS: A shriveled greyish-brown fungus also known as wood fungus; soak in warm water for 10 minutes.

CORNSTARCH: This fine white powder is widely used to thicken sauces. Mix cornstarch with an equal amount of water, add to the pan and cook, stirring constantly for a few seconds, until the sauce thickens and clears in color.

FIVE-SPICE POWDER: As the name implies, this is a mixture of five or more ground spices, including star anise, fennel, cloves, cinnamon and Sichuan pepper.

GALANGAL, LESSER: Lesser galangal (*san bai*) is a white, ginger-like rhizome believed to have medicinal properties. Do not confuse it with the fragrant greater galangal used in Southeast Asia. Look for it under the names "zedoary" or "krachai" (Thai). Omit if not available at Chinese medicine stores or Asian food stores.

GARLIC: Garlic is a very important ingredient in Chinese cuisine, not only for its flavor but for its medicinal properties. Garlic should be extremely finely chopped before cooking, unless otherwise specified in the recipes.

GINGER: Fresh ginger root is used in countless Chinese dishes and, like garlic, is valued for its medicinal properties. Scrape off the brownish skin and chop extremely finely, as for garlic. Some Cantonese cooks, especially those familiar with Hong Kong, use a touch of powdered ginger in one or two dishes; this is unconventional, but acceptable in some recipes as an addition to—never a replacement for—fresh ginger root.

GINSENG: A highly prized medicinal root, sometimes used in cooking; available in Chinese medicine shops. The root is expensive; packets of less costly fine side roots or shaved ginseng can be substituted.

HOISIN SAUCE: A sweet reddish-brown sauce made of soy beans used to season meat and also served as a dipping sauce. Sold in jars; keeps well if refrigerated after opening.

LOTUS: Dried **lotus nuts** should be soaked in boiling water for 1 hour, peeled, and the central core poked out with a thin skewer or toothpick. Canned lotus nuts normally have this hard core already removed. **Lotus root**, a tuber with a beige skin that should be removed, is popular for its crunchy texture and beautiful lacy pattern when sliced crosswise.

MONOSODIUM GLUTAMATE: Although this is out of favor in the West, cooks in China make wide use of this taste enhancer. If you use only top quality ingredients, there should be no need whatsoever for MSG.

MUSHROOMS, DRIED BLACK: Dried mushrooms, either dark black or deep brown in color, should be soaked in warm water for 20 minutes before use and the stems discarded. Do not substitute European dried mushrooms, as the flavor is different.

NOODLES: **Fresh noodles** (*mian*) are made from either wheat flour or rice flour and vary in thickness from round vermicelli-like threads to spaghetti, and from narrow to wide flat ribbons. Packs of **dried noodles** include wheat-flour noodles (sometimes with added egg); **dried rice vermicelli** and **mung-pea noodles**, also known as cellophane, jelly or transparent noodles.

OIL, COOKING: Blended vegetable oils (but never olive oil) are used by Chinese cooks for frying; **peanut oil** is sometimes specified for its distinctive flavor.

Lesser Galangal

Ginseng

Lotus Root

Giant White Radish

Preserved Salted Radish

Red Beans

Red Rice

Sichuan Pepper

ORANGE PEEL, DRIED: Dried orange peel is added to slow-cooked dishes for flavor. Although usually available in Chinese stores, fresh peel can be used as a substitute.

OYSTER SAUCE: Frequently added by Cantonese chefs to stir-fried vegetable dishes and meat, this sauce must be refrigerated after opening. If you do not like monosodium glutamate, choose your brand carefully, as most are laden with this controversial additive.

PRAWNS, DRIED: Used to add flavor to a number of dishes. Soak in warm water for about 5 minutes to soften, then discard any bits of hard shell.

PLUM SAUCE: Sold in cans or jars, this piquant reddish-brown condiment is made from salted plums, chilies, vinegar and sugar. Keep refrigerated after opening.

RADISH, GIANT WHITE: Sometimes known by its Japanese name (*daikon*) in the West, this is used either fresh as a vegetable or salted and pickled. **Preserved salted radish** keeps almost indefinitely on the shelf, and is often added to rice porridge (congee) and other dishes for its crunchy saltiness.

RED BEANS: Dried red azuki beans, smaller than kidney beans, are favored for dessert-type dishes. They are also cooked with sugar to make **red-bean paste**, a popular filling for buns and pancakes, usually sold in cans.

RED DATES: Valued for their medicinal properties as well as their prune-like flavor, these are added to soups and some other dishes. Soak in boiling water for 1 hour to soften before use.

RICE, RED: Very small reddish-brown grains, the leftovers from making rice wine, are used mainly for their red color.

ROCK SUGAR: Chunks of transparent rock sugar are preferred for certain desserts and drinks; they should be available in any Chinese store.

SALTED CABBAGE: Made from several types of cabbage, the most common being mustard cabbage, this is the Chinese equivalent of sauerkraut. It should be soaked in several changes of water for about 1 hour to remove excess saltiness.

SALTED SOY BEANS: Fermented, salted soy beans in a brownish sauce or paste are usually sold in jars. Mash slightly before using. They are sometimes confusingly labeled "Yellow Bean Paste." Some brands are already sweetened, but labeled accordingly. Sichuan brands contain additional chili. Keeps indefinitely on the shelf.

SESAME: Both **black** and **white sesame seeds** are used to flavor and add texture to a number of dishes. **Sesame oil** is used only as a seasoning, not as a frying medium. **Sesame paste** is made from ground toasted sesame seeds, unlike the Middle Eastern equivalent (*tahina*), which is made from untoasted seeds. Substitute smooth peanut butter.

SHALLOTS: Resembling clusters of tiny round red onions, these have a mild, sweet flavor.

SHARK'S FIN: Transparent threads of dried shark's fin (generally sold in packets) are highly valued for their gelatinous texture and are used in soups or sometimes cooked with egg. Soak in boiling water for about 30 minutes to soften before use.

SICHUAN PEPPER: This is not really pepper but a round, reddish-brown berry with a pronounced fragrance and flavor, used primarily in Sichuan cuisine and as an ingredient in five-spice powder. It is also known as prickly ash or fagara, and often sold powdered under the Japanese name, *sansho*.

SOY SAUCE: Three types are used in Chinese cooking. **Light soy sauce** is thinner, lighter in color and saltier than **black soy sauce**, which is often added to give a dark coloring to a dish. Delicately flavored **red soy sauce** is seldom used and can be substituted with light soy sauce.

SPRING ONION: Also known as scallion, the spring onion has slender stalks that are white at the base with dark green leaves. This is the most widely used herb in China.

STAR ANISE: A star-shaped brownish black spice with eight points, each containing a shiny seed, this has a pronounced aniseed fla-vor and is often cooked with beef.

SWEET SAUCE: There are several types of **black** and **red sweet sauce** used as a condiment or for seasoning food during cooking.

TARO: A starchy tuber, often with a faint pink appearance to the bland-tasting flesh, this is used both as a vegetable and in desserts.

VINEGAR: Black, red and white Chinese vinegars are all made from rice, and as the flavor differs, be sure to use the type specified. **White vinegar**, mild in flavor, is the most commonly used. **Red vinegar**, a light brown-ish red, has a distinctive tang, while full-bodied **black vinegar** has a faintly caramel flavor and is used sparingly as a seasoning or dip. Japanese rice vinegar makes an acceptable substitute for white vinegar; no good substitutes for red and black vinegar.

WATER CHESTNUT: Small crisp brown-skinned tubers with a crunchy texture and slightly sweet flavor.

WHITE FUNGUS: A crinkly golden-colored dried fungus that turns transparent after soaking, this is favored for its chewy texture.

YUNNAN HAM: Smoked salted ham, used mainly as a seasoning, Yunnan ham has a firm texture and excellent flavor. It is sold abroad in cans, although smoked Italian, French or Spanish ham could be substituted.

Star Anise

Taro

Water Chestnuts

White Fungus

Part Three: The Recipes

Basic recipes for pickles, sauces, dips and stocks precede those for the main dishes, which begin on page 38

PICKLES AND RELISHES

Pickled Radish and Carrot

1 small white radish, peeled
1 medium-sized carrot, peeled
2 teaspoons salt
1 red chili, deseeded
2 tablespoons sugar
2 tablespoons white rice vinegar

Cut the radish and carrot into matchstick pieces, put in a bowl and sprinkle with salt, stirring to mix well. Leave for 15 minutes, then squeeze to remove moisture. Cut the chili in very fine lengthwise shreds and add, together with sugar and vinegar, to the radish and carrot. Combine and chill before serving.

Hunan Chili Relish

5 red and 5 green chilies
5 cloves garlic
1 medium-sized onion
1 tablespoon oil
$^1/_4$ teaspoon salt

Coarsely chop chilies, garlic and onion. Heat oil and stir fry the chopped ingredients for 1 minute. Add salt and serve warm or at room temperature as an appetizer, or to accompany fried rice.

Ingredients

When a recipe lists a hard-to-find or unusual ingredient, see pages 27 to 31 for possible substitutes. If a substitute is not listed, look for the ingredient in your local Chinese or Asian food market, or check the mail-order listings on page 130 for possible sources.

Serving Sizes

As in almost all of Asia, food is seldom served in individual portions in China. As a general rule, the recipes in this collection will serve 4–6 people as part of a meal with rice and three other dishes.

Time Estimates

Time estimates are for preparation only and do not include actual cooking time.

⏱ *quick and very easy to prepare*

⏱⏱ *relatively easy; less than 15 minutes to prepare*

⏱⏱⏱ *takes more than 15 minutes to prepare*

Opposite:
Clockwise, from the top: Pickled Garlic, Spicy Cabbage Pickle, Marinated Cucumber, Pickled Radish and Carrot, Pickled Green Chili, Marinated Broccoli Stems and Peanuts (no recipe). Center: Hunan Chili Relish.

Pickled Green Chili

30 green chilies, sliced
4 cups white rice vinegar
1 teaspoon salt

Bring 2 cups of vinegar to a boil and scald the sliced chilies for 15 seconds. Drain and discard vinegar. Put chilies, remaining vinegar and salt in a dry glass jar. Cover and leave several days before eating with noodle dishes, or as an appetizer.

Marinated Broccoli Stems

Broccoli stems from 2 heads of broccoli
1 cup water
1 teaspoon salt
1 whole star anise
Pinch of dried chili flakes (optional)

Peel the broccoli stems and cut into strips ½-inch wide, 2½–3 inches long; this should fill 1 cup. Combine the broccoli stems with all other ingredients and marinate for 8 hours. Drain and serve as an appetizer.

Marinated Cucumber

1 cucumber, skin left on
3 tablespoons cooking oil
2 teaspoons finely chopped garlic
1 teaspoon sesame oil
1½ teaspoons sugar
½ teaspoon salt

Wash the cucumber, quarter lengthwise and discard seeds. Cut flesh into matchstick pieces and put in a bowl. Heat cooking oil and stir fry the garlic for a few seconds until it turns golden. Pour over the cucumber and mix in remaining ingredients. Chill and serve as a starter, or as an accompaniment to any cooked dish.

Pickled Garlic

3 cups water
6–8 complete garlic bulbs, skins left on
1 cup white rice vinegar
3 tablespoons sugar
1 teaspoon salt
1 bay leaf

Bring water to a boil in a pan, add the garlic and remove from the heat. Add remaining ingredients and leave to cool. Put garlic in a covered jar, top with liquid and marinate for 3 days before using. Drain and serve as an accompaniment or appetizer.

Spicy Cabbage Pickle

8 ounces long white Napa Chinese cabbage
1 tablespoon salt
3 red chilies, deseeded and shredded
1 inch ginger root, finely shredded
4 tablespoons sugar
4 tablespoons white rice vinegar
1 tablespoon cooking oil

Wash and dry cabbage leaves and cut into pieces about 2½ inches x ¾ inch. Put in a bowl, sprinkle with salt, mix and leave for 1 hour. Drain and discard any liquid. In a clean, dry bowl, combine cabbage with all other ingredients, except oil. Put into a clean glass jar. Heat oil and pour over the cabbage. When cool, cover tightly and marinate in the refrigerator for 2 days.

SAUCES AND DIPS

Ginger Garlic Sauce

1 ounce young ginger (4-inch piece)
6 cloves garlic
1 teaspoon salt
1 teaspoon sugar
1 teaspoon sesame oil
1 tablespoon cooking oil

Process ginger and garlic until fine. Combine with all other ingredients. Put in a covered jar and shake just before serving. Good with boiled meats.

Chili Garlic Sauce

5 red chilies, chopped
3 cloves garlic, chopped
3 tablespoons white rice vinegar
1 teaspoon sugar
$^1/_2$ teaspoon salt

Process all ingredients in a blender until fine. Keep refrigerated in a covered jar. Serve with steamed poultry or with rice and other cooked dishes.

Soy and Ginger Dip

2 teaspoons light soy sauce
2 tablespoons very finely chopped ginger
1 tablespoon finely sliced spring onion
$^1/_2$ teaspoon sugar
2 tablespoons peanut oil
1 tablespoon sesame oil

Combine soy sauce, ginger, spring onion and sugar. Heat both oils together until they smoke, then pour over the ginger mixture and stir. Serve immediately with steamed chicken or fish.

Ginger and Black Vinegar Dip

3-inch piece young ginger, scraped and very finely shredded
3 tablespoons black rice vinegar

Combine ginger and vinegar. Serve with Peking dumplings and other *dim sum* dishes.

Sesame Sauce

4 tablespoons sesame paste
4 tablespoons cold chicken stock (page 36)
1 teaspoon sesame oil
$^1/_2$ teaspoon salt
$^1/_2$ teaspoon sugar

Mix all ingredients well and serve with any seafood dish.

Hot Soy and Sesame Sauce

3 tablespoons light soy sauce
$2^1/_2$ tablespoons white rice vinegar
1 tablespoon Worcestershire sauce
1 tablespoon powdered Sichuan peppercorns or *sansho*
1 tablespoon finely sliced spring onion
1 teaspoon sesame oil

Mix all ingredients together in a bowl. Use to marinate meat or as a dip for steamed vegetables. (The use of Worcestershire sauce, an English ingredient, is unconventional and reflects the Chinese cook's willingness to adapt anything that might improve the flavor of food.)

Above:
Clockwise from top left: Sesame Sauce, Hot Soy and Sesame Sauce, Sichuan Pepper Oil, and Ginger and Black Vinegar Dip.

Sichuan Pepper and Salt Dip

**2 teaspoons powdered Sichuan peppercorns
  or *sansho***
1 teaspoon salt
¹⁄₂ teaspoon sugar

Combine and serve with Sichuan Duck, deep fried chicken and other poultry dishes.

Chili Oil

³⁄₄ cup peanut oil
1 tablespoon Sichuan peppercorns
2 dried chilies, sliced

Right:
Quail, hen and duck eggs, served either fresh, salted or preserved, are all enjoyed in China.
Opposite:
A selection of fresh and dried noodles. In some areas of China, fresh hand-pulled rather than machine-cut noodles are still prepared daily.

Heat wok and add oil, peppercorns and chilies. Cook over low heat for 10 minutes. Allow to cool, then store in a covered jar for 2–3 days. Strain and discard peppercorns and chilies. Store oil in a tightly sealed jar and keep in a cool place for up to 6 months.

Sichuan Pepper Oil

2 tablespoons Sichuan peppercorns
³⁄₄ cup peanut oil

Stir fry peppercorns in dry wok until fragrant. Add the oil and cook over low heat for 10 minutes. Allow to cool, then store in a covered jar for 2–3 days. Strain and discard peppercorns. Store oil in a tightly sealed jar and keep in a cool place for up to 6 months.

STOCKS

Gourmet Stock

1 pound pork ribs, blanched
12 ounces chicken pieces, blanched
12 ounces duck pieces, blanched
12 ounces smoked ham hock
2 spring onions, coarsely chopped
2 inches ginger root, sliced
¹⁄₄ cup Chinese rice wine
20 cups water

Combine all ingredients and simmer, uncovered, for 2 hours. Strain stock through cheesecloth.

Chicken Stock

**1 old hen or 3 pounds
  chicken pieces**
**1 celery stalk, with
  leaves still attached,
  chopped**
**2 inches ginger root,
  bruised**
10 cups water

Plunge the hen or chicken pieces into a large pan of boiling water and simmer for 1 minute. Discard water and refill pan with water and all other ingredients. Bring to a boil and simmer gently, uncovered, for 2 hours. Keep removing any scum or impurities as they rise to the top of the pan. Strain stock through cheesecloth. This can be made in large quantities and frozen in smaller portions for future use.

QING JIAO BAN PI DAN & LIANG BAN HUANG GUA

Century Egg with Pepper & Sichuan Cucumber with Dried Prawns

CENTURY EGG WITH PEPPER

Century eggs, with their strong flavor and melting texture, are partnered with green bell pepper in this simple, innovative Chinese recipe. ⏀

2 century eggs, peeled and cut in wedges
1 sweet green pepper, grilled until skin
   is slightly brown
$1/2$ tablespoon light soy sauce
$1/2$ teaspoon white rice vinegar
$1/2$ teaspoon peanut oil
$1/2$ teaspoon salt
$1/4$ teaspoon sugar
$1^{1}/_{4}$ inches ginger root, cut in hair-like shreds
1 red chili, deseeded and cut in hair-like shreds

Opposite:
*Sichuan
Cucumber with
Dried Prawns
(top left) &
Century Egg with
Pepper (right).*

Arrange the century eggs in a dish. Cut the grilled green pepper in wedges, discarding seeds. Combine soy sauce, vinegar, oil, salt and sugar, mixing well. Pour over the century egg and pepper and garnish with the shredded ginger and chili.

Helpful hint: Century eggs are known by several names, including 1000-year eggs and 100-year eggs.

SICHUAN CUCUMBER WITH DRIED PRAWNS

Simple and inexpensive to make, this appetizer gets its punch from the flavor of the dried prawns and Sichuan chili paste. ⏀

1 large or 2 small cucumbers, unpeeled
$1/2$ teaspoon salt
2 tablespoons dried prawns, soaked for
   5 minutes, then finely chopped
$1/2$–1 tablespoon Sichuan chili paste
$1^{1}/_{2}$ teaspoons light soy sauce
$1^{1}/_{2}$ teaspoons oil
Pinch of sugar

Cut the cucumber in four lengthwise pieces if large, or halve lengthwise if using long thin cucumbers (sometimes referred to as Japanese or Armenian cucumbers). Cut cucumber lengths on the diagonal to make attractive wedge-shaped pieces. Sprinkle with salt.

Combine all other ingredients in a mixing bowl, then add the cucumber and toss to blend well. Serve immediately.

GONG CAI XIAN SHEN PIAN & NU ER HONG NIU ROU

Duck Giblets & Marinated Sliced Beef

Opposite:
*Duck Giblets
(top right) and
Marinated Sliced
Beef (center).*

DUCK GIBLETS

Duck or chicken giblets, often discarded by Western cooks or relegated to the stockpot, are favored for their firm texture and flavor in China. The word *gong* in the name of this dish means gratuity to the emperor. ☻

- **10 ounces duck or chicken giblets**
- **2 teaspoons salt**
- **4 whole star anise**
- **4 bay leaves**
- **1 cup salted mustard cabbage, soaked, squeezed and sliced**
- **1 teaspoon sesame oil**

Clean the giblets and drain. Put in a pan with salt, star anise and bay leaves. Cover with water, bring to a boil and simmer for about 30 minutes until tender. Remove giblets, drain and keep refrigerated until required.

To serve, slice the giblets thinly, then mix with salted cabbage and sesame oil. If desired, garnish with a little sliced red chili. Serve cold.

MARINATED SLICED BEEF

Red rice (see page 30), which should be available in any Chinese medicine or specialty food shop, is used mainly to provide a touch of natural red coloring. It can, however, be omitted. ☻

- **12 ounces top round beef, in 1 piece**
- **2 teaspoons red rice (optional)**
- **2 tablespoons Chinese rice wine**
- **2 teaspoons salt**
- **4 bay leaves**

Put the beef in a pan with sufficient water to cover. Add all other ingredients and simmer, covered, until the beef is tender. Turn the meat from time to time and add a little more water if it threatens to dry up. Allow to cool. To serve, slice the beef thinly and arrange on a plate. Serve with a dipping sauce.

BAO BING

Fresh Spring Rolls

A favorite in the southeastern province of Fujian, these tasty rolls, made with fresh soft flour wrappers, are also known as *popiah* in some parts of Asia. If *popiah* or *bao bing* wrappers (also called Mandarin or *moo shu* pancakes) are not available, try using Filipino *lumpia* wrappers or make very thin pancakes from a thin batter of flour, egg and water. They won't be authentic *bao bing* skins, but the filling is so delicious that it won't matter. ☻☻☻

>   10 ounces small shrimp
>   1$\frac{1}{2}$ tablespoons lard or oil
>   2 squares hard bean curd, shredded
>   8 ounces lean pork, shredded
>   12 ounces bamboo shoots, shredded
>   1 large carrot, in matchstick pieces
>   5 cups shredded green cabbage
> $\frac{1}{2}$ cup snow peas, shredded lengthwise
>   1 tablespoon very finely minced garlic
> $\frac{1}{2}$ cup oysters, chopped if large (optional)
>   2 teaspoons salt
> $\frac{1}{2}$ teaspoon sugar
>   1 tablespoon Chinese rice wine
>   10–12 fresh spring roll skins (*bao bing*),
>   or *lumpia* wrappers
>   1 tablespoon blended mustard
>   1 tablespoon chili paste
> $\frac{1}{2}$ cup very finely shredded laver seaweed
>   2 tablespoons chopped cilantro leaf

Peel and devein shrimp. Put heads and shells into a pan with 3 cups of water and simmer 10 minutes. Strain through a sieve, pressing down on the heads and shells to extract the maximum stock. Set aside.

Heat lard or oil and fry shredded bean curd until golden. Add pork, shrimp and bamboo shoots and stir fry over moderate heat for 5 minutes. Add shrimp stock, cover and simmer over very low heat for 2 hours. Add the carrot, mix and simmer another hour. Add the cabbage and cook another 30 minutes, then put in the snow peas, garlic and oysters (if using). Simmer 5 minutes, then season with salt, sugar and rice wine. If the mixture threatens to dry up at any time, add water, a little at a time.

Just before the *bao bing* are required, spread a wrapper with mustard and chili paste to taste. Put in 2 heaped tablespoons of the cooked mixture, draining off any liquid first. Sprinkle with a little laver and cilantro, then roll up, tucking in the sides. Repeat until the filling is used up. Cut each *bao bing* crosswise into 3 or 4 pieces before serving.

Helpful hint: Japanese laver (*nori*) can be used if Chinese varieties are not available. This normally comes in sheets and can be shredded easily with a sharp knife.

CONG SHAO HUO CUI BING & CHAO LIAN XIA XIE JIAO

Ham-stuffed Pastries & Seafood in Bean Curd Skin

HAM-STUFFED PASTRIES ◷◷

Filling:

    8 ounces Yunnan or other smoked ham,
      in one piece
    1 cup finely sliced spring onion
    2 teaspoons sugar
    2 teaspoons sesame oil

Pastry:

    4 cups white flour
    6 tablespoons cooking oil
    2 teaspoons sesame oil
    About 1$\frac{1}{2}$ cups warm water

    Oil for deep frying

Opposite:
*Ham-stuffed
Pastries (on left of
the large serving
plate) and Seafood
in Bean Curd
Skin (on right of
serving plate).*

Steam ham for 30 minutes. Cool, then mince finely. Combine with other **filling** ingredients and set aside.

To make **pastry**, combine all ingredients and knead to form a pliable dough. Divide dough into two portions. Shape one portion into a ball and set aside. Roll the second portion of dough until about $\frac{1}{4}$ inch thick. Place the ball of dough in the middle and wrap it up with the flattened sheet of dough. Roll this larger ball into a flat sheet about $\frac{1}{4}$ inch thick.

Cut the dough into 3-inch squares. Put a tablespoonful of the filling into the center of each square and roll over to form a triangle or, if pre-ferred, fold into an envelope shape. Press the edges to seal firmly. Shallow fry each stuffed pastry in a little oil, turning once, until lightly golden. Drain, then deep fry in very hot oil for a few seconds until crisp and golden brown.

SEAFOOD IN BEAN CURD SKIN ◷◷

    6 ounces peeled shrimp
    4 ounces crabmeat, fresh or canned
    2 water chestnuts, roughly chopped
    1 tablespoon chopped cilantro leaves
    1 teaspoon salt
    3–4 large sheets of dried bean curd skin
    1 teaspoon cornstarch blended with water
    Oil for deep frying

Blend the shrimp and crabmeat in a food processor until coarsely chopped. Add water chestnuts, cilantro and salt and process for a few more seconds.

Wipe the bean curd skin with a damp cloth to make it pliable, then cut into 5-inch squares. Put in a heaped spoonful of filling and spread across. Smear the far end of the bean curd skin with cornstarch paste, then fold over the sides of the skin and roll up to seal the filling in firmly.

Deep fry in hot oil until crisp and golden. Cut rolls into bite-sized pieces before serving.

JIU SE CHAN HE

Nine Cold Cuts Combination

Chinese banquets usually begin with a plate of cold appetizers to sharpen the palate for the hot dishes to follow. These nine recipes illustrate different styles of Sichuan food preparation. You can serve as many or as few as you like as a starter to a Chinese meal.

STEAMED CHICKEN WINGS ☉☉

8 medium shrimp
1 teaspoon cornstarch
4 chicken wings, tips discarded and bones removed
1 tablespoon finely sliced spring onion
1/2 inch ginger root, finely sliced
1 teaspoon salt
1/4 teaspoon ground white pepper
2 tablespoons Chinese rice wine

Peel and devein the shrimp, discarding heads and shells. Chop or process the shrimp meat until fine. Mix with cornstarch and set aside. Put the chicken wings in a bowl with all remaining ingredients (except shrimp paste), mix well and leave to marinate for 10 minutes. Remove chicken wings from marinade, scraping off any spring onion and ginger. Stuff each chicken wing with shrimp paste and arrange on a plate. Steam for 8–10 minutes, allow to cool, then cut into 1/4-inch slices before serving.

STEAMED PORK WITH GARLIC ☉☉

8 ounces boneless pork shank
1/4 cup light soy sauce
1 teaspoon pounded garlic paste
2 teaspoons sugar
1 teaspoon chili oil (page 36)
1 teaspoon sesame oil

Steam pork in a covered bowl until tender. Cool, then slice as thinly as possible. Arrange on serving plate. Combine all other ingredients, mixing until sugar is dissolved, then pour over pork and serve.

DEEP-FRIED PORK WITH ORANGE PEEL ☉☉

8 ounces pork tenderloin or fillet, thinly sliced
1/2 cup Chinese rice wine
1 inch ginger root, finely sliced
1 tablespoon finely sliced spring onion
1 teaspoon salt
Oil for deep frying
2 dried chilies, cut in 1/4-inch pieces
1 strip dried orange peel, about 2 inches x 3/4 inch
1/2 cup gourmet or chicken stock (page 36)
1/4 cup sesame oil

Marinate the pork with wine, half the ginger, half the spring onion and salt for 30 minutes. Heat wok and add sufficient oil to deep fry the pork. Scrape

off any ginger and spring onion clinging to the pork, then deep fry meat until golden brown. Drain pork and pour out all but 1 teaspoon of oil.

Stir fry the dried chilies until reddish brown, then add remaining ginger, spring onion and orange peel, stirring well. Put in the stock and cook for 1 minute, then add pork and simmer for 2–3 minutes. Taste and add extra salt if desired, then stir in sesame oil. Leave pork to cool in the sauce and drain before serving.

SPICED CHICKEN ◔◑

1 chicken leg (thigh and drumstick)
$1/4$ cup light soy sauce
$1/4$ cup Chinese rice wine
1 tablespoon chili oil (page 36)
$1/2$ tablespoon sesame oil
$1/2$ teaspoon very finely chopped garlic
$1/2$ teaspoon very finely chopped ginger
1 teaspoon sesame paste or smooth peanut butter
$1/2$ teaspoon powdered Sichuan peppercorns or *sansho*
1 teaspoon finely sliced spring onion
$1/2$ tablespoon sesame seeds, toasted until golden

Simmer chicken leg in water to cover until cooked. Cool and debone, then slice the chicken thinly and arrange on serving plate. Put all other ingredients, except spring onion and sesame seeds, in a wok and bring to the boil. Simmer over low heat, stirring from time to time, for 10 minutes. Remove from heat and when cool, add the chicken. Serve chicken sprinkled with spring onion and sesame seeds (not shown in photograph).

FIVE-SPICED FISH ◔◑

10 ounces white fish fillets, sliced
1 teaspoon Chinese rice wine
1 teaspoon salt
1 tablespoon finely sliced spring onion
1 inch ginger root, finely shredded
Oil for deep frying
5 whole star anise
3-inch stick of cinnamon
1 dried red chili, cut in $1/2$-inch pieces
$1/2$ cup gourmet or chicken stock (page 36)
1 teaspoon sesame oil

Marinate the fish with rice wine, salt and half the spring onion and ginger for 15 minutes. Heat wok and add sufficient oil to deep fry the fish. Remove any marinade clinging to the fish and deep fry until golden. Remove and drain. Pour out all but 1 teaspoon of the oil, then add remaining ginger and spring onion, star anise, cinnamon and chili. Stir fry for a few seconds, then pour in stock and simmer for 5 minutes. Put in the fried fish and cook another 2 minutes. Add sesame oil and remove from heat. Let the fish cool in the sauce and drain before serving.

RABBIT WITH FRUIT JUICE ◔◑

10 ounces rabbit leg, deboned and cut in $1/2$-inch cubes
$1^1/2$ inches ginger root, finely sliced
1 tablespoon finely sliced spring onion
1 teaspoon salt
Oil for deep frying
$1/2$ cup gourmet or chicken stock (page 36)
1 cup pineapple juice
1 cup orange juice

Marinate rabbit with ginger, spring onion and salt for 15 minutes. Heat sufficient oil in a wok for deep frying the rabbit. Remove any marinade clinging to the rabbit and deep fry until golden. Remove and drain. Clean the wok, add stock and the fruit juices. Simmer for 5 minutes, then add the fried rabbit and simmer for 5 minutes. Leave to cool in the sauce and drain just before serving.

BOILED PORK TONGUE ◷◷

5 ounces pork tongue
2 teaspoons Sichuan pepper oil (page 36)
2 cups gourmet or chicken stock (page 36)
1 teaspoon salt
1 tablespoon spring onion
2 teaspoons peanut or salad oil

Simmer the tongue in water to cover until tender. Allow to cool, then slice. Heat wok and add Sichuan pepper oil, stock and salt. Simmer until reduced by half, then put in tongue. Remove from heat and allow to cool. Toss the spring onion and peanut oil in a bowl. To serve, drain the tongue and put on a plate, garnished with the tossed spring onion.

SESAME SQUID ◷◷

5 ounces squid, skinned and cleaned
1 cup water
1 teaspoon salt
1 tablespoon sesame paste
2 teaspoons sesame oil

Cut the squid in pieces about 2 inches x $\frac{3}{4}$ inch. Score crosswise in a diamond pattern with a sharp knife, cutting about halfway into the squid meat so that it will curl during cooking. Bring water and salt to a boil and drop in squid. Simmer just until the squid turns white and curls (about 1 minute), then drain.

Combine sesame paste and oil in a mixing bowl and add squid. Toss and serve at room temperature or chilled, if preferred.

CARROT AND RADISH ROLLS ◷

1 large carrot, shredded
$2\frac{1}{2}$-inch piece giant white radish, peeled and sliced
3 teaspoons sugar
2 teaspoons white rice vinegar
2 teaspoons sesame oil
$\frac{1}{2}$ teaspoon salt

Blanch the carrot and radish separately in a little boiling water. Drain well and pat dry with paper towel. Place the slices of radish flat on a board and put some shredded carrot crosswise in the center of each. Roll up to enclose the carrot, then cut each roll on the diagonal into pieces of about $\frac{1}{2}$ inch.

Arrange on a plate. Combine all remaining ingredients, mixing until the sugar dissolves. Pour over the rolls and serve.

DONG GUA TANG

Winter Melon Soup

A restaurant classic appreciated as much for the showy presentation of the winter melon—invariably beautifully carved—as for the clear, clean flavor of the stock. Winter melon is believed to be very *yin*, cleansing and cooling for the body and good for the skin. As the predominant flavors of this creation are chicken stock and the delicate winter melon, be sure to use either gourmet stock or good fresh chicken stock rather than bouillon cubes. ☯ ☯

> 1 large winter melon
> 1 teaspoon salt
> 6 cups gourmet or chicken stock (page 36)
> 4 ounces straw mushrooms, halved
> $\frac{1}{3}$ cup shredded cooked chicken breast
> $\frac{1}{3}$ cup shredded cooked duck meat (or double the amount of chicken)
> $\frac{1}{3}$ cup shredded cooked liver (duck, chicken or pork)
> $\frac{1}{4}$ cup cooked or canned crabmeat
> $\frac{1}{4}$ cup canned asparagus tips, drained
> 6 dried lotus nuts, soaked, peeled and hard core removed
> Salt to taste

Choose a winter melon that will hold at least 6 cups liquid. Cut off the top or, if the melon is very large, slice it in half. Carve the skin decoratively. Remove central fiber and seeds. Scrape out some of the flesh, leaving about $\frac{3}{4}$ inch flesh still clinging to the skin. Sprinkle the inside with salt and put winter melon in a large deep pan with boiling water to cover. Simmer for 30 minutes, drain and then put in a large steamer and steam for another 30 minutes.

Bring the stock to a boil and pour into the melon. Cover and steam for 25 minutes. Add all other ingredients and serve. Add some of the winter melon flesh, scraped out with a spoon, when serving the soup in individual bowls.

Helpful hint: You will need a large saucepan to simmer the winter melon. If your steamer is not deep enough to hold the melon for the final stage of cooking, put a rack or plate on two or three small bowls set on the bottom of a large saucepan and add water. Sit the winter melon on the rack above the surface of the water.

GOU JI NIU WEI TANG

Clear Oxtail Soup

A subtle, light soup, with box thorn berries—believed to make the eyes brighter—adding goodness and flavor. Blanching the oxtail for about 3 minutes before adding it to the remaining ingredients gets rid of any traces of fat and any impurities. ⊘

6 slices (about 1½ inches thick) meaty oxtail, fat removed, blanched in boiling water
2 spring onions, cut in 3-inch lengths
2 inches ginger root, finely sliced
½ cup Chinese rice wine
2 teaspoons salt
1 tablespoon box thorn berries
½ teaspoon ground white pepper

Put blanched oxtail, spring onions, ginger, wine and salt in a pan and cover oxtail with water. Cover pan, bring to a boil, then simmer gently until the oxtail is very tender. Just before serving, add the box thorn berries and sprinkle with pepper. Serve in individual bowls with one piece of oxtail per serving.

TAI HU YIN YU GENG & SHEN JI CHONG CAO DUN YA

Tai Lake Whitebait Soup & Duck Soup with Herbs

TAI LAKE WHITEBAIT SOUP

Fresh whitebait, poetically referred to as "silver fish," are found in Tai Hu Lake, near Wu Xi, an area famed for its natural beauty. Shredded white-fleshed fish could be used as a substitute, although nothing matches the flavor of fresh whitebait. ☻

*Tai Lake
Whitebait Soup
(left) and Duck
Soup with
Herbs (right).*

- 2 cups chicken stock (page 36)
- 4 ounces fresh whitebait or smelts, or white fish fillets, shredded
- 2-inch piece bamboo shoot, in matchstick shreds
- 2 pieces cloud ear fungus, soaked and finely shredded
- 1 dried black mushroom, soaked and finely shredded
- 2 tablespoons shredded soft bean curd
- $1/2$ teaspoon salt
- 2 teaspoons cornstarch, blended with water

Bring stock to a boil, then add all ingredients except cornstarch. Simmer for a minute or two, until the whitebait or fish is cooked. Thicken with cornstarch and serve immediately. If desired, garnish with a little cilantro leaf.

DUCK SOUP WITH HERBS

Medicinal herbs are often cooked with chicken to make a soup that is regarded as being more important for its restorative value than its flavor. This duck soup, with ginseng, box thorn berries, lesser galangal and caterpillar fungus, tastes excellent as well as reputedly being good for the kidneys, lungs, eyes and general health. ☻

- $1^{1}/_{2}$ pounds duckling
- 10 cups chicken stock (page 36)
- 1 tablespoon sliced dried lesser galangal (*san bai*) (optional)
- $3/4$ ounce ginseng root
- $3/4$ ounce caterpillar fungus
- $3/4$ ounce box thorn berries
- 2 teaspoons salt
- 1 teaspoon ground white pepper

Soak the duckling in tepid water for 30 minutes to remove any impurities. Drain duckling, then put in a large bowl with all other ingredients. Cover the bowl, place inside a steamer and steam for 2 hours. To serve, cut the duckling into individual portions and serve in soups bowls with stock and some of the herbs added for garnish.

YU CHI TANG

Shark's Fin Soup

The use of shark's fin demonstrates the ingenuity of Chinese cooks, who believe almost anything is edible. The fins are dried and sold either whole or shredded and come in a great variety of grades, with top quality ones costing up to thousands of dollars. Shark's fin is a real gourmet item, enjoyed for its texture and its ability to absorb the flavors of other ingredients. 🕐 🕐

1 ounce shredded dried shark's fin
3 cups gourmet or chicken stock (page 36)
3 teaspoons black soy sauce
$\frac{1}{2}$ teaspoon salt
$\frac{1}{4}$ teaspoon ground white pepper
$1\frac{1}{4}$ inches ginger root, very finely shredded
$\frac{1}{3}$ cup finely shredded cooked chicken
2 tablespoons cornstarch, blended with water
1 teaspoon shallot oil (see Helpful hint below)
$\frac{1}{3}$ ounce (10 g) dried scallops (optional)
$\frac{1}{3}$ ounce (10 g) dried fish maw (optional)
$1\frac{1}{2}$ cups chicken stock (optional)
1 teaspoon dry sherry (optional)
$\frac{1}{2}$ inch ginger root, sliced (optional)
1 stalk spring onion (optional)
1 heaped tablespoon finely shredded
  Yunnan ham

Soak dried shark's fin in hot water for about 30 minutes until swollen and transparent. Drain.

Heat stock with soy sauce, shallot oil, salt and pepper, then add shark's fin, scallops, fish maw, ginger and chicken. Thicken with cornstarch and serve. Garnish with shredded Yunnan ham. In southern China, a few drops of black rice vinegar are generally added to the soup at the table.

The scallops and fish maw depicted in the photograph opposite are optional, and may be ready-bought in dried form. To prepare the scallops, place them in a bowl containing chicken stock, dry sherry, ginger root and spring onion. Steam in a steamer until the scallops are soft.

To prepare the fish maw, place them in a bowl, pour enough hot water over to soak them, cover with a lid, and set aside until soft.

Helpful hint: To make shallot oil, peel and slice about 8 shallots. Heat 1 cup of oil, add the shallots and simmer in the oil until the shallots are golden. Do not allow the shallots to burn or the flavor will be bitter. Drain and store the oil in a jar with a tight-fitting lid.

HAI XIAN SUAN LA TANG

Hot Sour Soup

This tangy Sichuan favorite combines seafood in the form of sea cucumber and shrimp with dried mushrooms, fungus and bean curd; some cooks, however, prefer to substitute chicken and pork for the seafood. The heat of this soup comes from ground white pepper rather than chilies. ☺ ☺

$^1/_2$ **sea cucumber**
2 cups chicken stock (page 36)
5 large peeled shrimp, diced
1$^1/_2$ tablespoons thawed frozen green peas
1 dried black mushroom, soaked and
    finely diced
2 pieces cloud ear fungus, soaked and
    finely diced
$^1/_2$ **cake soft bean curd, finely diced**
$^1/_2$ **medium-sized tomato, finely diced**
1 teaspoon salt
3 teaspoons ground white pepper
1 teaspoon sesame oil
2 tablespoons cornstarch, blended with water
1 egg, lightly beaten
2 tablespoons black rice vinegar
1 tablespoon finely sliced spring onion

Soak the sea cucumber in hot water until soft, then cut in half lengthwise. Clean the interior and dice the flesh finely.

Heat the stock and add sea cucumber, shrimp, peas, mushroom, fungus, bean curd and tomato. Bring to a boil, then simmer for 1 minute. Add salt, pepper and sesame oil. Thicken the soup with cornstarch, then add the egg and stir until set. Add the vinegar, pour into a serving bowl and garnish with spring onion.

HONG TANG DAN DAN MIAN

Hot and Spicy Hawker Noodles

It's hard to think of any time of day when noodles are not popular in China; they're eaten for breakfast, as a mid-morning snack, for lunch, as something to keep you going until dinner and as a late-night restorative. This spicy favorite, often sold by mobile vendors or at streetside stalls, originates in Sichuan. ☻ ☻

1 pound fresh wheat-flour noodles, or
$^3/_4$ pound narrow flat dried noodles
1 teaspoon cooking oil
8 ounces lean pork, very finely minced
$^1/_2$ cup preserved salted radish, finely chopped
2 cups chicken stock (page 36)
4 tablespoons black soy sauce
1$^1/_2$ tablespoons black rice vinegar
1 tablespoon very finely chopped garlic
2 teaspoons Sichuan pepper oil (page 36)
2 teaspoons sesame oil
1 teaspoon chili oil (page 36)
1 teaspoon ground white pepper
1 heaped tablespoon finely sliced spring onion

Set the noodles aside for blanching later. Heat cooking oil and stir fry the pork over very high heat for 2–3 minutes, until cooked. Mix well with the preserved radish and set aside.

Heat chicken stock and add all other ingredients except noodles and spring onion. Keep stock warm while blanching noodles in rapidly boiling water for 1 minute.

Drain noodles and divide among 4 small bowls. Pour over hot stock, top with the pork mixture, garnish with spring onion and serve.

CHAO MIAN XIAN

Fried Noodles Xiamen Style

Very fine fresh wheat-flour noodles, like angel-hair pasta, are used for this dish popular in the southern coastal province of Fujian. Choose whatever noodles are available, but do try to get fresh ones as the texture is superior to dried noodles. ☺☺

10 ounces small shrimp
1 pound fresh wheat-flour noodles
Oil for deep frying
2 tablespoons very finely chopped garlic
7 ounces bamboo shoots, in matchstick shreds
4 ounces lean pork, finely shredded
1 small carrot, in matchstick shreds
3–4 dried black mushrooms, soaked and finely shredded
$1/4$ cup chopped Chinese coarse chives
2 tablespoons Chinese rice wine
1 teaspoon salt
$1/2$ teaspoon ground white pepper
4 shallots, sliced and deep fried until golden brown

Peel shrimp, remove heads and devein. Keep shrimp aside and put heads and shells in a pan with 1 cup water. Bring to a boil, then simmer 10 minutes. Strain through a sieve, pressing on heads and shells to extract the maximum stock. Set aside.

Shake the noodles to separate if using fresh noodles, then deep fry in hot very oil for a few seconds until golden brown. Drain well and set aside, discarding oil. If using dried noodles, blanch in boiling water until just softened.

Put 1 tablespoon of fresh oil into the wok, stir fry the garlic for a few seconds, then add the shrimp, bamboo shoots, pork, carrot, mushrooms and chives. Stir fry until the pork and shrimp change color. Pour in $1/2$ cup of the reserved shrimp stock, add wine, salt and pepper and simmer, uncovered, for 5 minutes, stirring from time to time.

Add the fried or blanched noodles and continue stir frying, mixing well, for another 5 minutes. Serve garnished with fried shallots.

CHUAN WEI HUN TUN

Boiled Dumplings in Hot Sauce

Steamed or boiled dumplings are a favorite snack in most of China, from Beijing in the north to Shanghai on the east coast, from the southern province of Guangdong to Sichuan in the far west. The filling differs from one area to another, as well as according to the season. In summer time in Beijing, the basic pork stuffing might be seasoned with fresh dill. The dumplings may be steamed, fried, boiled, served in soup (like the famous Cantonese *won ton* soup) or, as in this Sichuan version, bathed in a tangy sauce. ☺ ☺

50 fresh *won ton* wrappers
8 ounces lean pork, finely minced
1 egg, lightly beaten
1½ teaspoons very finely chopped ginger root
2 tablespoons Chinese rice wine
1 teaspoon salt
¼ teaspoon ground white pepper

Sauce:

1 teaspoon finely chopped garlic
4 tablespoons black soy sauce
½ teaspoon sugar
½ teaspoon ground cinnamon
4 tablespoons chili oil (page 36)
1 tablespoon finely sliced spring onion

Most *won ton* wrappers are 3–4 inches square. Turn a small Chinese soup bowl or a glass upside down on the wrappers and cut around the bowl or rim of the glass with a sharp knife to form circles.

Combine pork, egg, ginger, rice wine, salt and pepper. Put a heaped teaspoonful of this in the center of a wrapper. Use your fingertip to smear a little water around the edge of the circle, then fold across to make a semicircle, pressing firmly to enclose the filling. When all the dumplings are ready, drop in rapidly boiling water and simmer for 2–3 minutes. Drain.

Take 4 bowls and prepare the sauce separately for each portion. Put ¼ teaspoon garlic, 1 tablespoon black soy sauce, a pinch of sugar and a pinch of cinnamon in the bottom of each bowl. Divide the boiled dumplings among the 4 bowls and pour 1 tablespoon chili oil over each serving. Garnish with a little spring onion. Stir before eating.

CHENGDU LENG MIAN

Cold Chengdu Noodles

If you've always eaten piping hot noodles, this dish might seem a little surprising. However, chilled noodles are a popular summer dish in China as well as in neighboring Japan. This dish is quick and easy to prepare; boil the noodles in the morning, chill them for a few hours, combine the sauce and you have an almost instant luncheon. ⏱

1 pound fresh wheat-flour noodles, boiled, drained and chilled
3/4 cup bean sprouts, blanched for a few seconds and chilled
1 spring onion, finely sliced

Sauce:

2 tablespoons very finely chopped ginger root
1 tablespoon very finely chopped garlic
1 tablespoon sesame paste
1 tablespoon peanut butter
1 teaspoon peanut oil or cooking oil
3 tablespoons black soy sauce
2 teaspoons sugar
2 teaspoons black rice vinegar
1 teaspoon sesame oil
1 teaspoon chili oil (page 36)

Combine all **sauce** ingredients in a bowl, mixing well. Add the noodles and stir to coat the noodles with the sauce, then add bean sprouts and mix carefully with chopsticks or a fork, taking care not to break the sprouts. Divide among 4 bowls and sprinkle each portion with a little spring onion.

CHAO ZHOU CHAO FAN & SU CHAO FAN

Teochew Fried Rice & Vegetarian Fried Rice

TEOCHEW FRIED RICE ☺☺

4 cups cold cooked rice
3 teaspoons cooking oil
2 eggs, lightly beaten
8 large peeled shrimp, diced
2 ounces squid, diced
2 ounces chicken or duck, diced
2 ounces fish fillet or pork, diced
2 ounces Chinese sausage, sliced
$1/2$ cup mustard green stalks or spring onion,
    cut in $1^1/2$-inch lengths
1 teaspoon salt

Break up the rice grains with a fork and set aside. Heat 1 teaspoon of the oil in a wok. Pour in the beaten eggs and cook until set, then push with a frying spatula to break into pieces. Remove and set aside.

Heat remaining 2 teaspoons of oil. Stir fry all other ingredients, except rice and salt, over maximum heat for 2 minutes. Add rice and salt, then stir fry for another 2 minutes. Mix in the fried egg and serve immediately.

VEGETARIAN FRIED RICE ☺☺

4 cups cold cooked rice
1 cake hard bean curd
1 teaspoon black soy sauce
3 tablespoons oil

3 spears fresh asparagus, or 3 green (French)
    beans, cut in $3/4$-inch pieces
1 tablespoon salted black beans
1 tablespoon boiled green mung peas
1 tablespoon boiled red azuki beans
$1/2$ cup bean sprouts
1 teaspoon salt
Ground white pepper to taste
3 red chilies, deseeded and chopped
3 green chilies, deseeded and chopped
3 cloves garlic
$1/2$ medium-sized onion, finely chopped

Break up the rice grains with a fork and set aside. Cut the bean curd in half crosswise, then shred and marinate with the soy sauce for a few minutes. Heat 1 tablespoon oil in a wok and stir fry the bean curd until crisp. Set aside.

Heat 1 tablespoon fresh oil and stir fry the asparagus, three types of beans and sprouts over high heat for 1 minute. Add the rice, increase heat to the maximum and stir fry for about 1 minute, until the rice is heated through. Season with salt and pepper and put on a serving dish.

Put the remaining tablespoon of oil in the wok and gently fry the chilies, garlic and onion for about 1 minute. Put this in the center of the fried rice and surround with the fried shredded bean curd. Serve immediately.

MA LA LIAN OU & XIE HUANG XIAN ZHU SUN

Lotus Root Salad & Bamboo Shoots with Crab Roe

LOTUS ROOT SALAD

The lotus has special associations for Buddhists, for it is said that Gautama Buddha likened man striving to achieve goodness to an exquisite lotus bloom rising unsullied from the muddy bottom of a lake. ☉

1 section of lotus root, about 6–8 inches long
1 tablespoon white rice vinegar
2 tablespoons sugar
Salt to taste

Opposite:
*Lotus Root Salad.
Photograph of
Bamboo Shoots
with Crab Roe is
on page 73.*

Peel the lotus root and cut crosswise into slices about $\frac{1}{4}$-inch thick. Heat a pan of water until boiling, then drop in the lotus root slices and blanch for about 5 seconds. Drain and rinse in cold water.

Toss the lotus root slices in a bowl with the vinegar, then arrange on a plate. Sprinkle with sugar and salt to taste and serve immediately.

BAMBOO SHOOTS WITH CRAB ROE

Bamboo shoots are decoratively cut to resemble a flower in this beautiful vegetable composition. ☉ ☉

1 pound bamboo shoots
8 large peeled shrimp
Pinch of salt
2 teaspoons cornstarch
1 tablespoon water

2 ounces fresh crab roe (or substitute any
**   fresh roe)**
$\frac{1}{4}$ cup chicken stock (page 36)
8 ounces spinach leaves

Trim off and discard the sides of the bamboo shoots to make long rectangles. Using a very sharp small knife, cut a "V" shape on each side of the rectangle and pry off the piece of bamboo shoot, which will resemble a flower.

Mince or blend together the shrimp, salt, 1 teaspoon of cornstarch and water. Put a small amount of this mixture into the center of each bamboo "flower" and top with a tiny dab of roe. Arrange on a plate and steam over high heat for 3–4 minutes.

While the bamboo shoots are steaming, bring a pan of boiling salted water to a boil and blanch the spinach leaves until tender. Drain. When the bamboo shoots are ready, put on a serving plate and surround with the spinach leaves. Heat chicken stock and thicken with the remaining teaspoon of cornstarch blended with water. Pour over the bamboo shoots and serve immediately.

Helpful hint: If you find it difficult to make the flower shapes, slice the bamboo shoot crosswise and mound the shrimp paste and crab roe on the top, although the final result will not be as decorative.

DOU FU JIA XIANG NIANG & DOU FU ROU JIANG ZHA

Deep-fried Savory Bean Curd & Pork-stuffed Steamed Bean Curd

Bean curd, make from the "milk" pressed from cooked, protein-rich soy beans, is available in many forms and is very versatile, as these recipes demonstrate.

DEEP-FRIED SAVORY BEAN CURD ☺☺

1 pound bean curd
1 cup white flour
1 egg, beaten
2 teaspoons chicken stock powder
$\frac{1}{2}$ teaspoon salt
$\frac{1}{2}$ teaspoon sugar
1 heaped tablespoon chili paste or sauce
Water to mix
4 ounces finely minced lean pork
Oil for deep frying
$\frac{1}{4}$ teaspoon ground white pepper

Cut bean curd into pieces about 3 inches long and $\frac{3}{4}$ inch wide. Set aside. Combine all other ingredients except pork, oil and pepper to make a batter the consistency of a thick cream. Mix in pork. Heat oil in a wok until almost smoking. Dip the pieces of bean curd, one by one, into the batter and turn carefully with the fingers until well coated. Put into the oil and deep fry for about 3–4 minutes until golden brown. Sprinkle with pepper and serve immediately.

PORK-STUFFED STEAMED BEAN CURD ☺☺

1 pound bean curd
3 teaspoons cornstarch
4 ounces finely minced lean pork
3 dried black mushrooms, soaked and finely chopped
2 teaspoons chicken stock powder
$\frac{1}{2}$ teaspoon salt
1 teaspoon sugar
1 teaspoon Chinese rice wine
$1\frac{1}{2}$ cups leafy greens (spinach, Napa cabbage or *bok choy*), blanched
$\frac{1}{2}$ cup chicken stock (page 36)

Cut the bean curd into squares of about 3 inches x $1\frac{1}{2}$ inches thick. Use a teaspoon to scoop out some of the bean curd from the center to make a hole for the pork filling. Combine 1 teaspoon cornstarch with all other ingredients, except leafy greens and stock, mixing well. Stuff this into the bean curd and steam over high heat for 4 minutes.

While the bean curd is steaming, cook the greens in chicken stock. Drain, keeping the stock. Arrange greens on a plate. Blend remaining 2 teaspoons cornstarch with water and thicken the stock. Pour over vegetables, arrange the cooked bean curd on top and serve.

MA PO DOU FU & BEI GU SU

Spicy Bean Curd with Minced Beef & Bean Curd with Vegetables

SPICY BEAN CURD WITH MINCED BEEF

Although beef is included in this dish, the dominant ingredient is meltingly soft bean curd laced with pungent Sichuan seasonings. ⏱⏱

1 pound soft bean curd
3 tablespoons oil
4 ounces minced lean beef
1 tablespoon salted black beans
1 tablespoon chili paste
1 tablespoon salted soy beans
1 tablespoon very finely chopped ginger root
1 teaspoon very finely chopped garlic
2–3 spring onions, finely sliced
1 cup chicken or beef stock
1 tablespoon black soy sauce
$\frac{1}{2}$ teaspoon salt
2 teaspoons cornstarch, blended with water
1 teaspoon powdered Sichuan peppercorns or *sansho*

Cut the bean curd in $\frac{3}{4}$-inch dice. Heat oil and stir fry beef and black beans for 3–4 minutes. Add chili paste, salted soy beans, ginger, garlic and spring onions. Stir fry for another 2 minutes, then add the stock and bean curd.

Simmer for 5 minutes, season with soy sauce and salt, then thicken with cornstarch. Sprinkle with Sichuan pepper and serve.

BEAN CURD WITH VEGETABLES ⏱

1 pound hard bean curd
Oil for deep frying
$\frac{1}{2}$ cup baby *bok choy* (*bai cai*), blanched
$\frac{1}{2}$ carrot, sliced and cut in flower shapes, blanched
3 dried black mushrooms, soaked
1 teaspoon chicken stock powder
2 teaspoons oyster sauce
$\frac{1}{2}$ teaspoon Chinese rice wine
$\frac{1}{2}$ teaspoon sugar
$\frac{1}{4}$ cup chicken stock (page 36)
1 teaspoon cornstarch, blended with water

Cut the bean curd into 3-inch lengths. Deep fry in very hot oil until golden, then drain. Pour out all but 2 teaspoons of oil and return the bean curd with blanched vegetables, mushrooms and seasoning. Stir fry for about 1 minute, then add chicken stock and heat through. Thicken with cornstarch and serve immediately.

Opposite:
Spicy Bean Curd with Minced Beef. Photograph of Bean Curd with Vegetables is on page 73.

XIA MI CHAO HUANG GUA & XIANG GU CHAO JIAO BAI

Cucumber with Dried Prawns & Bamboo Shoots with Mushrooms

CUCUMBER WITH DRIED PRAWNS

Dried prawns add a special flavor to normally bland cucumbers in this dish from the coastal province of Fujian, famous for its fresh and dried seafood. ⏱

- **1 large cucumber (12 ounces)**
- **2 teaspoons oil**
- **1 teaspoon very finely chopped garlic**
- **4 ounces dried prawns, soaked to soften**
- **1 teaspoon chicken stock powder**
- **1 teaspoon Chinese rice wine**
- **1 teaspoon sugar**
- **$\frac{1}{2}$ teaspoon salt**
- **1 teaspoon cornstarch, blended with water**
- **1 red chili, finely shredded for garnish (optional)**

Do not peel cucumber. If using the long, very thin variety, cut in half lengthwise; if using fatter cucumbers, quarter lengthwise. Remove seeds and cut cucumber pieces on the diagonal into $1\frac{1}{2}$-inch lengths.

Heat oil in a wok and stir fry the garlic and dried prawns for about half a minute, until fragrant. Add the cucumber and all other ingredients, except cornstarch and chili. Stir fry for 2–3 minutes, then thicken the liquid that exudes from the cucumbers with cornstarch. Serve garnished with chili, if desired.

BAMBOO SHOOTS WITH MUSHROOMS

The special type of bamboo shoot used for this dish in southern China has an excellent texture and flavor somewhat reminiscent of fresh heart of palm. Unless you are lucky enough to live where fresh *jiao bai* is available, substitute canned bamboo shoots. ⏱

- **12 ounces *jiao bai* or bamboo shoots**
- **2 teaspoons oil**
- **1 heaped teaspoon very finely chopped garlic**
- **10 dried black mushrooms, soaked**
- **1 teaspoon Chinese rice wine**
- **1 teaspoon chicken stock powder**
- **1 teaspoon sugar**
- **$\frac{1}{2}$ teaspoon salt**

If using fresh *jiao bai*, peel off the outer layer, then slice coarsely. If using canned bamboo shoots, simmer in boiling water for 5 minutes, drain and slice coarsely.

Heat oil in a wok and stir fry the garlic and mushrooms until fragrant. Add the *jiao bai* or bamboo shoots and all seasonings and stir fry for 1–2 minutes. Serve immediately.

GUANG DONG NIANG SAN BAO
Stuffed Vegetables and Bean Curd

This Cantonese and Hakka favorite uses a selection of vegetables and bean curd stuffed with a shrimp filling. The sauce, flavored with salted black beans, gives an emphatic salty tang to the delicate stuffed vegetables. ⏱ ⏱

1 large sweet green pepper
1 long thin eggplant
1 hard bean curd cake
1 teaspoon cornstarch
Oil for deep frying

Stuffing:

8 ounces peeled shrimp, chopped (1 cup)
$\frac{1}{4}$ cup lard, chopped
1 tablespoon black moss fungus,
    soaked to soften
$\frac{1}{2}$ teaspoon salt
Dash of ground white pepper

Sauce:

1 teaspoon salted black beans, mashed slightly
    with the back of a spoon
1 teaspoon finely chopped red chili
1 teaspoon very finely chopped garlic
1 teaspoon very finely chopped ginger root
1 cup chicken stock (page 36)
$\frac{1}{2}$ teaspoon black soy sauce
2 teaspoons cornstarch, blended with water

Prepare the **stuffing** first by blending together all ingredients. Set aside.

Cut the green pepper into four and discard seeds. Cut the eggplant across into $1\frac{1}{2}$-inch lengths and make a lengthwise slit down one side to form a pocket for the stuffing. Cut bean curd into four and slit a pocket in each. Sprinkle the inside of the vegetables and bean curd with cornstarch to help make the stuffing adhere, then fill with the stuffing.

Heat oil in a wok and deep fry the stuffed items, a few at a time, until golden and cooked. Remove and set aside, leaving 1 teaspoon of oil in the wok for preparing the sauce.

To make the **sauce**, stir fry the black beans, chili, garlic and ginger for a few seconds until fragrant, then add the stock and soy sauce. Heat, then add the fried vegetables and bean curd and simmer for 1 minute. Thicken with cornstarch and serve immediately.

Helpful hints: Other vegetables that can be used include bitter gourd and green or red chilies with the seeds removed. The stuffing can be prepared in advance and the vegetables cleaned (although not cut and stuffed) to save time.

YU XIANG QIE ZI & SHANG TANG LU SUN

Fragrant Eggplant with Pork & Quick-cooked Asparagus

FRAGRANT EGGPLANT
WITH PORK ☺☺

8 ounces eggplant, peeled and cut in pieces
  3 inches x $^1/_2$ inch
Oil for deep frying
2 ounces ground lean pork ($^1/_4$ cup)
2 tablespoons dried prawns, soaked and
  very finely chopped
2 teaspoons chili paste
1 teaspoon salted soy beans, mashed
2 teaspoons very finely sliced spring onion
1 teaspoon very finely chopped soaked dried
  black mushroom
1 cup chicken stock (page 36)
1 teaspoon Chinese rice wine
1 teaspoon sesame oil
2 teaspoons commercial sweet and sour sauce
$^1/_2$ teaspoon dark soy sauce
$^1/_4$ teaspoon salt
1 teaspoon cornstarch, blended with water
Cilantro leaves to garnish

Deep fry the eggplant pieces in very hot oil for 1 minute. Drain and set aside.

Pour out all but 2 teaspoons of the oil and stir fry pork over high heat for 2 minutes. Add dried prawns, chili paste, salted soy beans, 1 teaspoon of the spring onion and the mushrooms. Stir fry for 30 seconds, then add all remaining ingredients, except remaining spring onion, cornstarch and cilantro.

Heat, then put in eggplant and cook another 30 seconds. Thicken with cornstarch and serve garnished with the cilantro leaves and remaining spring onion.

QUICK-COOKED ASPARAGUS ☺

4 ounces fresh asparagus spears (about 4)
Oil for deep frying
1 cup water
$^1/_4$ teaspoon salt
$^1/_4$ teaspoon sugar
$^3/_4$ cup chicken stock (page 36)
1 teaspoon Chinese rice wine
$^1/_4$ teaspoon sesame oil
1 teaspoon cornstarch, blended with water
1 tablespoon finely shredded Yunnan ham

Trim off the hard ends of the asparagus and dry the spears thoroughly. Heat oil in a wok and deep fry the asparagus over very high heat for just 15 seconds. Drain and set aside. Discard oil.

Bring water, salt and sugar to a fast boil in the wok and blanch the asparagus for 15 seconds, or slightly longer if using thick asparagus spears. Pour off the water and add stock, wine and sesame oil to the asparagus. Bring to a boil, then thicken with cornstarch. Serve garnished with the ham.

CHAO QING CAI & CHAO ZHOU ZHENG CHANG YU

Stir-fried Mixed Vegetables & Teochew Steamed Pomfret

Opposite:
Teochew Steamed Pomfret (left) with marrow and prawns (no recipe). Photograph of Stir-fried Mixed Vegetables is on page 81.

STIR-FRIED MIXED VEGETABLES ⊘

$^1/_2$ cup snow peas, ends trimmed
2 teaspoons oil
Pinch of salt
$^1/_4$ teaspoon sugar
3 ounces bamboo shoots, quartered lengthwise then cut in 2-inch lengths
6–8 dried black mushrooms, soaked
1 cup chicken stock (page 36)
1 teaspoon oyster sauce
$^1/_4$ teaspoon sesame oil
$^1/_4$ teaspoon salt
$^1/_4$ teaspoon dark soy sauce
Dash of ground white pepper
1 teaspoon cornstarch, blended with water

Blanch snow peas in boiling water for 5 seconds, then drain. Heat oil and stir fry blanched snow peas with salt and sugar for 30 seconds. Remove from wok. Add bamboo shoots, mushrooms, chicken stock and all seasonings and bring to a boil. Simmer 1 minute, add the snow peas, then thicken with cornstarch. Serve immediately.

TEOCHEW STEAMED POMFRET

The Chao Zhou (also know as Chiu Chow or Teochew) of southern China are known for their light, non-greasy food and especially for their delicate touch with seafood. This recipe for steamed pomfret demonstrates the subtlety of this style of cooking. ⊘ ⊘

1 fresh pomfret, pompano, butterfish or plaice, about $1^1/_2$ pounds
$^1/_2$ cup salted mustard cabbage, soaked and finely sliced
1 tomato, deseeded and cut in strips
2 sour salted plums (available in jars)
1 red chili, deseeded and finely shredded
3-inch celery stalk, finely shredded
1 spring onion, chopped in $1^1/_2$-inch lengths
3 inches ginger root, finely shredded
1 cake bean curd, shredded
1 dried black mushroom, soaked and finely shredded
2 teaspoons chicken stock powder
$^1/_2$ teaspoon sugar
$^1/_4$ teaspoon salt
Cilantro leaf to garnish

Clean the fish inside and out and wipe dry. Place fish on an oval plate and arrange over it all the ingredients, except chicken stock powder, sugar and salt. Sprinkle with the stock powder, sugar and salt and put inside a large steamer. Steam over high heat for about 8 minutes, until the fish is cooked. Take care not to overcook for optimum texture and flavor. Garnish with cilantro leaf.

YU XIANG CUI PI GUI YU

Crispy Fried Mandarin Fish

The Chinese believe that freshwater fish from lakes, rivers and fish ponds are more delicate in flavor and texture than fish from the sea. Although this recipe calls for freshwater Mandarin fish, fine-textured ocean fish such as perch, grouper, bream or snapper could be substituted. ☻☻

1 fresh fish (see above), 1¹/₂–2 pounds, cleaned and scaled
3 inches ginger root, finely sliced
1 spring onion, chopped coarsely
1 teaspoon ground white pepper
¹/₂ cup Chinese rice wine
2 tablespoons cornstarch
Oil for deep frying
1 spring onion, finely sliced for garnish

Sauce:
1–2 tablespoons chili paste
1¹/₂ teaspoons finely chopped garlic
1¹/₂ teaspoons finely chopped ginger root
1¹/₂ teaspoons white rice vinegar
1 teaspoon sugar
¹/₂ teaspoon salt
³/₄ cup chicken stock (page 36)
1 spring onion, finely sliced
2 teaspoons cornstarch, blended with water

Cut 4 or 5 deep diagonal slashes on each side of the fish to help it cook more quickly. Marinate the fish for 15 minutes with ginger, chopped spring onion, pepper and rice wine. Drain fish and scrape off any pieces of the marinade. Dry thoroughly.

Heat a wok and add oil. When the oil is hot, sprinkle the fish on both sides with cornstarch, shaking it to remove any excess. Carefully lower the fish into the oil and cook, over moderate heat, for about 5–8 minutes until golden brown and cooked through. Drain and keep warm on a serving dish.

Discard all but 1 teaspoon of the frying oil. To prepare the **sauce**, stir fry the chili paste, garlic and ginger for a few seconds until fragrant, then add all other ingredients, except cornstarch. Simmer for 2 minutes, then thicken with cornstarch. Pour the sauce over the fish and garnish with spring onion. Serve immediately.

CU JIAO YU

Poached Fish

Mandarin fish, carp or other freshwater fish are preferred for this dish in China. Trout would be a good substitute, although ocean fish such as perch, seabass or grouper could also be used. Do not attempt this dish unless you can be sure of spanking fresh fish, for like all other steaming or poaching recipes, where the seasonings are subtle, the quality of the fish is vital. ⊘

1 whole fresh fish (see above), 1½–2 pounds, scaled and cleaned
3 spring onions, shredded
2 pieces ginger root, each about 2 inches long, finely shredded
1 red chili, deseeded and shredded
2 tablespoons Chinese rice wine
2 tablespoons white rice vinegar
1 teaspoon salt
½ teaspoon ground white pepper
½ cup peanut or cooking oil

Put sufficient water to cover the fish in a wok and add half the spring onion and half the ginger. Bring to a boil, reduce heat and add the fish. Simmer very gently until the fish is cooked.

While the fish is cooking, combine the wine, vinegar, salt and pepper in a mixing bowl and set aside. When the fish is tender, remove, drain and put on a serving plate. Garnish with the remaining spring onion, ginger and chili and pour over the prepared mixture. Heat the oil until smoking in a wok and pour over the poached fish. Serve immediately.

Helpful hint: The use of oil with poached fish might seem strange, but it is a common technique in China and adds a very special flavor.

SONG GUO YU

Deep-fried Carp with Sweet and Sour Sauce

A sweet and sour sauce with deep-fried fish or pork is a Chinese restaurant cliché throughout the world, so it might come as a surprise to learn that even in China, this classic is still very popular. In this recipe, the fish flesh is removed in fillets, then cut to give it a diamond pattern so that it curls when cooked. This technique also ensures that the maximum amount of fish meat is in contact with the tangy sauce. ✪✪

1 whole fresh carp, perch, grouper, snapper or
   bream, $1\frac{1}{2}$–2 pounds
1 cup cornstarch
Oil for deep frying

Sauce:

3 tablespoons tomato paste
$\frac{1}{2}$ cup water
$\frac{1}{2}$ teaspoon salt
3 tablespoons sugar
2 teaspoons white rice vinegar
1 heaped tablespoon frozen green peas,
   defrosted
1 teaspoon cornstarch, blended with water

Clean and scale the fish. Carefully remove the flesh from both sides of the fish, keeping the head, backbone and tail intact. Leave the skin on the fish fillets but remove all bones carefully. Put the fish fillets, skin side down, on a chopping board. Using a sharp knife, carefully cut diagonal lines across each piece of fish, taking care not to cut right through to the skin. Turn the fish and cut diagonal lines across those already made to form a diamond pattern. Cut the fish fillets into pieces about $2\frac{1}{2}$ inches x $\frac{3}{4}$ inch and set aside.

Heat oil in a wok until very hot. Sprinkle the fish skeleton on both sides with cornstarch, shaking to remove any excess. Deep fry the skeleton until lightly brown and crisp, then drain and arrange on a serving plate. Dip the prepared pieces of fish in cornstarch, shaking to remove any excess, then deep fry in the same hot oil until crisp and golden brown. Drain and arrange on top of the fish skeleton.

Tip the oil out of the wok and add all **sauce** ingredients, except cornstarch. Bring to a boil, lower heat, then thicken with cornstarch. Taste and add more vinegar, if desired. Pour sauce over the fish and serve immediately.

PI PA XIA

Pi Pa Shrimp

This dish is fancifully named after the *pi pa*, a classical Chinese stringed instrument, which the shrimp are thought to resemble. Whole shrimp are dipped into a blended shrimp paste and steamed. They can be set aside for a few hours and deep fried just before serving. ② ②

12 large shrimp, about 2½–3 inches long
Oil for deep frying
1 egg white, lightly beaten
2 tablespoons cornstarch
12 small Chinese wine cups or egg cups

Shrimp Paste:

10 ounces shrimp
6 tablespoons lard, diced
1 dried black mushroom, soaked and
  finely chopped
1 tablespoon finely chopped bamboo shoot
  or water chestnut
1 teaspoon salt
2 egg whites
2 tablespoons cornstarch

Sauce:

1 cup chicken stock (page 36)
1 teaspoon rice wine
Salt to taste
2 teaspoons cornstarch, blended with water

Prepare the **shrimp paste** first. Peel the shrimp, discarding heads, tails and shells. Devein. Process shrimp in a blender for a few seconds with the diced lard. Add all other shrimp paste ingredients and process just until well blended. Grease tiny Chinese wine or egg cups with a little oil, then divide the shrimp paste among these, packing it in firmly.

Peel the medium shrimp, discarding heads and shells but leaving on the tail for a more decorative appearance. Push the head end of each shrimp into a paste-filled cup, leaving the tail end protruding. Repeat until all the shrimp are used up, then steam for 20 minutes. Allow to cool, then remove from the cups with the tip of a knife.

Just before the dish is required, prepare the **sauce** by bringing stock, wine and salt to a boil. Thicken with cornstarch and keep warm.

Heat oil for deep frying in a wok. Dust each steamed shrimp with a little cornstarch, dip into the egg white and deep fry until golden brown. Put on a serving dish and pour the sauce over the top.

YU ZAN XIA REN

Hairpin Shrimp

Slivered vegetables encircled with shrimp are thought to resemble the long hair pins that are traditionally pushed through a twist of hair, hence the name "Hairpin Shrimp." ⊘ ⊘

8 medium-sized prawns, about 2½–3 inches in length
1 teaspoon baking soda
¼ teaspoon salt
¼ teaspoon sesame oil
½ cup julienned Chinese mustard green stalks or spring onions
½ cup julienned carrots
½ cup julienned bamboo shoots
½ cup julienned Yunnan ham
Oil for deep frying
Dash of ground white pepper

Sauce:
4 tablespoons chicken stock (page 36)
1 tablespoon Chinese rice wine
¼ teaspoon salt
¼ teaspoon sesame oil
1 teaspoon cornstarch, blended with water

Peel the shrimp, discarding heads, tails and shells. Cut down the back of each shrimp and devein. Flatten shrimp open and marinate with baking soda, salt and sesame oil for 20 minutes.

Cut the mustard green stalks, carrots, bamboo shoots and ham into slivers about twice the thickness of a matchstick, 2½ inches in length. Use the tip of a sharp knife to slash a hole about ½ inch from the head end of the shrimp, and another hole ½ inch from the tail end. Take one sliver each of mustard green stalk, carrot, bamboo shoot and ham and, holding them together, push through one slit of the shrimp. Fold the shrimp into a semicircle so you can push the vegetables out through the second slit, pressing the shrimp together firmly to hold the filling.

Heat water in a wok and when boiling rapidly, blanch the vegetable-filled shrimp for 10 seconds. Remove and drain. Pour out the water, dry the wok and heat oil for deep frying. Deep fry shrimp over very high heat for 30 seconds, then drain and arrange on a serving plate.

Tip out all but 1 tablespoon of oil and add all **sauce** ingredients, except for cornstarch. Bring to the boil, lower heat and thicken with cornstarch. Pour over the shrimp, sprinkle with pepper and serve immediately.

ZENG CHENG BAI HUA NIANG XIAN GUO

Shrimp-stuffed Lychees

A fine example of the creativity and delicacy of Cantonese food, this decorative dish combines fresh lychees—regarded by most Chinese as the ultimate fruit—with a simple minced shrimp filling. The texture of fresh lychees is best. However, if you cannot obtain fresh lychees, use canned fruit, but rinse well to remove any sugar syrup. ⊘⊘

8 ounces peeled shrimp, finely chopped or blended (1 cup)
1 teaspoon salt
1 teaspoon cornstarch
¼ teaspoon ground white pepper
10 fresh or canned lychees, peeled and stones removed
Few lettuce leaves for garnish
Cilantro leaf to garnish
Chili flakes to garnish (optional)

Sauce:
1 cup chicken stock (page 36)
1 teaspoon cooking oil
½ teaspoon salt
1 teaspoon cornstarch, blended with water
2 egg whites

Mix together the shrimp, salt, cornstarch and pepper. Divide mixture in 10 portions. Sprinkle the inside of each lychee with a dusting of additional cornstarch and stuff with the shrimp paste, pushing it in well. Put the lychees on a plate and steam over high heat for 6–8 minutes, until the shrimp filling is firm and cooked.

Arrange lettuce leaves in a shallow bowl and put the lychees on top. Prepare **sauce** by bringing stock, oil and salt to a boil. Lower heat and thicken with cornstarch, then stir in the egg white and remove from the heat. Pour over the lychees and serve immediately.

YOU BAO YOU YU JUAN

Squid with Bamboo Shoots

Squid is very popular in coastal regions of China, and like all seafood, the fresher it is, the better the flavor. As is common in Asia, Chinese cooks often score the squid so that it has an attractive "pine cone" appearance after cooking. ☻☻

- **1 pound fresh squid, peeled and cleaned**
- **Oil for deep frying**
- **1 teaspoon finely chopped garlic**
- **3 ounces bamboo shoots, thinly sliced lengthwise in 2-inch pieces**
- **¼ cucumber, thinly sliced lengthwise in 2-inch pieces**
- **1 carrot, thinly sliced lengthwise in 2-inch pieces**
- **1 spring onion, sliced**
- **2 tablespoons Chinese rice wine**
- **1 teaspoon salt**
- **1 teaspoon cornstarch, blended with water**

Cut the cleaned squid in half lengthwise and score each piece with a sharp knife in a diamond pattern, taking care not to cut right through the flesh. Cut the scored squid into pieces about 2½ inches x ¾ inch. Dry thoroughly.

Heat oil and when very hot, deep fry the squid for 5 seconds only. Drain and set aside. Pour out all but 1 teaspoon of the oil and reheat it. Stir fry the garlic for a few seconds until fragrant, then add the squid and stir fry for 1 minute. Add the bamboo shoots, cucumber, carrot and spring onion and stir fry for 1 minute. Season with rice wine and salt, then thicken with cornstarch. Serve immediately.

SUAN RONG ZHENG DAN CAI

Steamed Mussels with Minced Garlic

This way of cooking mussels can be used also for oysters or clams. The shellfish are boiled just until they open, then steamed with seasonings and topped with a garnish of fried garlic, spring onion, chili and cilantro leaf. Very simple and also very good. 🕐 🕐

12 fresh mussels or oysters, or 24 clams
6–8 cloves garlic
1 teaspoon oil
1 teaspoon chicken stock powder
1 teaspoon sugar
¹/₂ teaspoon light soy sauce
1 red chili, finely chopped
1 spring onion, finely sliced
Cilantro leaf (optional)

Bring a wok full of water to a boil. Put in mussels or other shellfish and cook until the shells open. Remove, drain, and discard one side of the shell. Put the half-shell with the mussel attached on a plate.

Slice half the garlic and fry gently in oil until crisp and golden. Drain and set aside. Chop the remaining garlic very finely and scatter a little over each of the mussels. Sprinkle them with chicken stock powder, sugar and soy sauce. Put inside a steamer and cook over high heat for 3 minutes.

Garnish with the fried garlic, chili, spring onion and cilantro and serve immediately.

Helpful hint: The shellfish can be boiled in advance and kept in the refrigerator until you are ready to steam them.

Opposite:
Clockwise from top left: Steamed Mussels around rim of plate, with Steamed Oysters in the center, uncooked clams, uncooked bamboo oysters and Steamed Clams.

JIAO XIAN XIA GU & XIANG JIAO CHAO XIE

Baby Slipper Lobsters & Fried Chili Crab

BABY SLIPPER LOBSTERS

Flathead or slipper lobsters (known as *cigale de mer* in France and as Balmain or Moreton Bay bugs in Australia) are found in both the Mediterranean and Indo-Pacific regions. Not only are the mature lobsters eaten along the southeastern Chinese seaboard, but tiny immature lobsters are deep fried, head, tails, shells and all. Large shrimp could be used as a substitute. ☻

Opposite:
Baby Slipper
Lobsters (left)
and Fried Chili
Crab (right).

1 pound baby slipper lobsters or large shrimp
Oil for deep frying
2 teaspoons finely chopped garlic
1 teaspoon salt
1 teaspoon ground white pepper
1 red chili, finely chopped

Wash and dry the baby lobsters or shrimp, but do not peel. Deep fry in hot oil for 3–4 minutes until golden brown. Remove and drain. Discard all but 2 teaspoons of oil. Stir fry the garlic for a few seconds until fragrant, then add the fried lobsters and all other ingredients. Stir fry for a few seconds and serve immediately.

FRIED CHILI CRAB

This recipe comes from Fujian province in southeastern China. ☻

1 pound flower or other type of crab
Oil for deep frying
1 tablespoon finely chopped garlic
20 dried chilies, left whole but stalks cut off
1 small sweet green pepper, in fine strips
4 ounces lean pork, finely shredded
$\frac{1}{2}$ cup water
3 tablespoons oyster sauce
$\frac{1}{2}$ teaspoon chicken stock powder
$\frac{1}{2}$ teaspoon salt
1 tablespoon sugar
2 teaspoons cornstarch, blended with water

Pull off the backs of the crabs, discard spongy grey matter inside and wash. Use a cleaver to chop the body, legs still attached, into four pieces. Smash the claws lightly with a cleaver to allow the sauce to penetrate. Dry crab thoroughly.

Heat oil and deep fry the crab for 5–7 minutes, then drain and set aside. Remove all but 2 teaspoons of oil from the wok and stir fry the garlic, chilies, green pepper and pork over moderate heat for 2–3 minutes until the pork has changed color. Add crab and all other ingredients, except cornstarch, and simmer for 1 minute. Thicken with cornstarch and serve.

LONG FENG CHENG XIANG

Stir-fried Lobster with Chicken in Hot Sauce

This elaborate dish is considered very auspicious as the shape of the lobster is thought to resemble the powerful dragon, while the chicken is reminiscent of the immortal phoenix. ☺☺☺

Stir-fried Lobster:

 1 medium-sized lobster, meat diced, shell boiled
 $\frac{1}{2}$ teaspoon salt
 Pinch of sugar and pepper
 1 egg white
 1 tablespoon cornstarch, blended with water
 2 tablespoons oil
 $\frac{1}{2}$ sweet red pepper, shredded
 2 dried black mushrooms, soaked and shredded
 4–5 snow peas, ends trimmed, cut lengthwise
 $\frac{1}{2}$ teaspoon finely chopped garlic
 $\frac{1}{2}$ teaspoon finely chopped ginger
 $\frac{1}{4}$ teaspoon salt
 Pinch of sugar and pepper
 1 tablespoon Chinese rice wine
 1 tablespoon chicken stock (page 36)
 1 teaspoon cornstarch, blended with water

Season the lobster meat with salt, sugar, pepper, egg white, cornstarch and 1 tablespoon oil, massaging to mix well. Heat remaining tablespoon of oil and stir fry the lobster for 5 seconds, then add red pepper, mushrooms and snow peas. Continue cooking over high heat for 1 minute. Add garlic and ginger, stir to mix well, then add all remaining ingredients,

except cornstarch. Heat through, thicken with cornstarch and keep warm while preparing the chicken.

Chicken in Hot Sauce:

 8 ounces boneless chicken, diced
 $\frac{1}{2}$ teaspoon salt
 Pinch of pepper
 $\frac{1}{2}$ cup cornstarch, blended with water
 Oil for deep frying
 $\frac{1}{2}$–1 tablespoon chili paste
 1 tablespoon finely chopped garlic
 1 tablespoon finely chopped ginger root
 $\frac{1}{4}$ cup chicken stock (page 36)
 1 tablespoon black rice vinegar
 1 tablespoon sugar
 2 teaspoons light soy sauce
 $\frac{1}{4}$ cup Chinese rice wine
 2 teaspoons cornstarch, blended with water
 $1\frac{1}{2}$ cups steamed broccoli

Sprinkle chicken with salt, pepper, cornstarch and 2 teaspoons of cooking oil, massaging to mix well. Deep fry chicken for 3–4 minutes until crisp and golden. Drain and set aside. Discard oil. Heat 1 tablespoon fresh oil and fry the chili paste for a few seconds. Add garlic and ginger and stir fry for a few seconds, then add all other ingredients, except blended cornstarch and steamed broccoli. Heat through, thicken with cornstarch. Serve chicken and lobster on a platter, garnished with steamed broccoli.

QI GAI JI

Beggar's Chicken

According to legend, this dish was created by a poor man who stole a chicken. He was about to cook it on a fire when the landowner passed by. To conceal it, he hastily wrapped the chicken in mud and tossed it on the fire. Later, when the danger had passed, he broke open the mud casing to find a succulent cooked bird inside. This more refined version includes stuffing that the beggar would never have been able to lay his hands on, and encases the chicken in an edible bread dough rather than mud.
🕐🕐🕐

1 fresh chicken, about 3 pounds, cleaned
2 dried lotus leaves

Stuffing:

5 ounces pork, finely shredded
3 ounces preserved dried vegetable
  (*mei cai*), finely chopped
5 dried black mushrooms, soaked and shredded
3 inches ginger root, finely shredded
1–2 spring onions, finely sliced
2 teaspoons chicken stock powder
2 teaspoons sugar
2 teaspoons light soy sauce
3 tablespoons rice wine
Pinch of powdered ginger

Dough Wrapping:

8 cups white flour
4 teaspoons dried yeast
2 tablespoons sugar
1 tablespoon salt
2 eggs, beaten
2 cups warm water

Make the **dough wrapping** first. Sift flour into a bowl, add all other ingredients and mix well to make a pliable dough. Add a little more water or flour if necessary to achieve the right consistency. Cover and leave to rise while preparing chicken.

Combine all ingredients for the **stuffing**, mixing well. Stuff the chicken and close each end with a strong toothpick. Wrap in the lotus leaves, overlapping to enclose the chicken. Put on a plate and steam over high heat for 30 minutes.

Knead the dough and roll out into a rectangle large enough to enclose the chicken. Put steamed chicken in the dough and close, pinching well to seal. Bake at 375°F until the dough is golden brown (about 15 minutes). Cut open at the table and serve the chicken and stuffing. The dough can also be eaten.

Helpful hint: If lotus leaves are unavailable, substitute parchment paper.

CUI PI SHAN DONG JI

Deep-fried Shandong Chicken

Like many Chinese recipes, this dish from the north-eastern province of Shandong involves two methods of cooking: the chicken is first simmered very gently, then deep fried. It is served with a clear, non-thickened sauce with a slightly hot and sour edge to it. ☻ ☻

1 fresh chicken, about 2$\frac{1}{2}$ pounds
2 teaspoons salt
Oil for deep frying
1 spring onion, white part only, shredded
2 cloves garlic, finely chopped and deep fried

Sauce:

1 red chili, deseeded and sliced
4 cloves garlic, sliced
1 teaspoon chili paste
$\frac{1}{2}$ cup white rice vinegar
1 cup chicken stock (page 36)
1 tablespoon light soy sauce
$\frac{1}{2}$ teaspoon salt

Rub the chicken inside and out with salt and set aside for 30 minutes. Bring a large pot of water to a boil and put in the chicken. Lower heat to the minimum and simmer the chicken for 30 minutes. Drain the chicken, pat dry and hang in an airy place to dry thoroughly.

Just before the dish is required, heat oil for deep frying in a wok. To ensure a crisp texture, make sure the chicken is thoroughly dry (a brief session with a hair dryer sometimes helps). Lower the whole chicken, breast side down, into the oil and fry for about 5 minutes until golden brown. Turn and fry the other side for another 5 minutes. Remove chicken from oil, drain, chop into bite-sized pieces and arrange on a serving dish deep enough to contain 1$\frac{1}{2}$ cups sauce.

Tip out all the oil from the wok but do not wipe. Add the **sauce** ingredients and simmer for 2 minutes. Pour over the chicken and garnish with spring onion and fried garlic.

Helpful hints: Chinese cooks usually cook the bird with the head still on, serving this on the plate; the serving of the head, however, is entirely optional. This is a useful dish that can be partially prepared in advance; simmer and dry the chicken and keep for several hours before the final frying.

GONG BAO FENG HUA & MAN TOU

Chicken with Dried Chilies & Steamed Dumplings

CHICKEN WITH DRIED CHILIES ☺☺

5 ounces chicken breast
½ teaspoon salt
1 egg white
2 tablespoons Chinese rice wine
2 teaspoons cornstarch
Oil for deep frying
1 teaspoon finely chopped garlic
1 teaspoon finely chopped ginger
1 tablespoon black soy sauce
1 tablespoon white rice vinegar
1 teaspoon sugar
2–3 dried chilies, cut in ½-inch pieces,
    dry-fried until crisp and lightly browned
1 tablespoon finely sliced spring onion
2 tablespoons fried peanuts, skinned

Opposite:
Chicken with
Dried Chilies.
Photograph of
Steamed
Dumplings
is on page 111.

Score chicken breast with diagonal cuts about ¼ inch apart, taking care not to cut right through the flesh. Cut the breast into pieces about ¼ inch x ¾ inch. Mix well with salt, egg white, wine and cornstarch. Set aside for 2–3 minutes while heating oil for deep frying. Deep fry chicken over very high heat for 30 seconds, drain and set aside.

Tip out all but 1 teaspoon of oil from the wok. Stir fry the garlic and ginger for a few seconds, then add soy sauce, vinegar and sugar. Stir well and put in the chicken, dried chilies and spring onion and and stir fry for 3–4 minutes. Stir in the fried peanuts and serve immediately.

STEAMED DUMPLINGS ☺☺

2 cups white flour, sifted
½ tablespoon sugar
2 teaspoons dried yeast
1 teaspoon baking powder
½ cup warm water
1 teaspoon oil

Combine all ingredients except oil, adding a little more water if needed to make a smooth pliable dough. Knead for a couple of minutes, then cover and set aside for 20 minutes until doubled in size. Knead the dough for 1 minute. Pinch off lumps of dough about the size of a golf ball and roll out on a floured board to circles about 3 inches in diameter.

Brush the center of each circle with a touch of oil so that the dumpling will open easily after steaming. Fold the circle across to make a semicircle, then fold again into quarter circle. Use the tines of a fork to cut two slashes about ¼ inch long on the curved edge of the dough, so the dumpling will resemble a flower after steaming. Steam dumplings over high heat for 4–5 minutes and serve with Sichuan Smoked Duck (page 110).

ZHANG CHA YA

Sichuan Smoked Duck

Peking duck is one of the most famous Chinese duck preparations, although many connoisseurs prefer the Sichuan style of smoking the duck before frying it. Morsels of cooked duck and spring onions are tucked into moist steamed dumplings smeared with a tangy sauce. ⏱⏱⏱

1 fresh duck
1 tablespoon salt
1 teaspoon powdered Sichuan peppercorns
    or *sansho*
3 spring onions, coarsely chopped
3 inches ginger root, sliced
$\frac{1}{2}$ cup Chinese rice wine
$\frac{3}{4}$ cup black Chinese tea leaves
$\frac{1}{2}$ cup sugar
$\frac{1}{2}$ cup bay leaves
4 whole star anise
2 sticks cinnamon, each 3 inches in length
4–6 spring onions, white part only, shredded

Sauce:

$\frac{1}{2}$ cup *hoisin* sauce
1 teaspoon Sichuan peppercorn powder
    or *sansho*
1 teaspoon sesame oil
$\frac{1}{2}$ teaspoon salt
$\frac{1}{4}$ teaspoon sugar
1 teaspoon oil

Wash the duck thoroughly and pat dry. Sprinkle the duck inside and out with salt and Sichuan pepper, massaging well. Put half the chopped spring onions and half the ginger inside the duck, then put the duck in a bowl and sprinkle with remaining spring onions and ginger. Pour over the rice wine and leave to marinate for 45 minutes.

Remove the duck from the marinade. Heat a wok full of water and when it is boiling, lower the bird into the wok and use a large ladle to scoop the water over the duck. Blanch for 1 minute, drain and leave to dry while preparing the smoking ingredients.

Mix tea leaves, sugar, bay leaves and star anise in a bowl, then put into the wok with the cinnamon. Heat over a moderate fire, stirring, for 2–3 minutes, then put a rack over the smoking ingredients. Put the duck on the rack, cover the wok and smoke the duck over low heat for 1 hour.

Stir together all the **sauce** ingredients and put in individual bowls. Put spring onion into individual bowls.

When the duck has been smoked, remove from the wok, discarding the smoking ingredients. Heat oil for deep frying and fry the smoked duck over very high heat, turning to cook all over to a golden brown. Drain, cut into serving pieces and serve with Steamed Dumplings (page 108), sauce and spring onions.

SHUAN YANG ROU

Mongolian Lamb Hot Pot

When the Mongolians from the north invaded China, they brought with them their taste for mutton. Their legacy is still found in Beijing today, although mutton is disliked in almost all other areas of China, except the western autonomous provinces. Mongolian Hot Pot is popular in winter time and as a reunion dinner, with everyone sitting around in a cozy warm circle, cooking their own portions of food in the bubbling hot pot. ⏱⏱

> 1 pound boneless lamb leg
> 1–2 cakes bean curd, sliced
> 3 cups Napa cabbage, coarsely chopped
> 4 ounces dried rice vermicelli, soaked in hot water to soften

Stock:
> 1¼ inches ginger root, finely sliced
> 1 spring onion, coarsely chopped
> 2 teaspoons dark soy sauce
> 6 cups stock made from lamb leg bone boiled with water

Dips and Garnishes:
> ½ cup sesame paste
> 2 tablespoons fermented bean curd, mashed
> ½ cup light soy sauce
> ½ cup red rice vinegar
> ½ cup Chinese rice wine
> ¼ cup chili oil (page 36)

4 tablespoons pickled garlic (page 34)
Bunch of cilantro leaf, chopped

Slice the lamb paper thin, leaving on a little of the fat (this is typical in Beijing, but can be omitted if preferred). Roll up the slices and arrange on a plate. Put the bean curd and cabbage on separate plates, and divide the soaked vermicelli among 6 individual soup bowls.

Arrange all **dips and garnishes** in small bowls and place on the table for diners to use according to taste.

Heat all **stock** ingredients in a pan, then carefully transfer to a hot pot. Bring back to a boil. Each diner cooks his own portions of meat, bean curd and cabbage, seasoning them afterwards with the dip of his choice, accompanied by pieces of pickled garlic and cilantro. When all the ingredients are used up, the rich stock is poured into the soup bowls over the noodles and eaten as a final course.

Helpful hint: The hot pot is a type of fondue traditionally heated by charcoal, although electric and gas models are also available. If using a charcoal hot pot, light charcoal over a gas flame and then use tongs to insert it down the central chimney of the hot pot and into the bottom. Protect your table surface by putting the hot pot on a thick wooden chopping board.

HUI GUO ROU

Twice-cooked Pork with Peppers

Sweet red and green peppers add color and a contrasting texture to this excellent recipe, where the pork is flavored with salted black beans, chili and fragrant *hoisin* sauce. It's an excellent way of using any leftover roasted, steamed or boiled pork. ◷

1 large or 2 small sweet red peppers
1 large or 2 small sweet green peppers
Oil for deep frying
8 ounces cold cooked pork, thinly sliced
2–3 teaspoons chili paste
1 teaspoon *hoisin* sauce
1 heaped tablespoon salted black beans, rinsed
**   and lightly mashed**
2 teaspoons finely chopped garlic
2 teaspoons finely chopped ginger root
2 teaspoons black soy sauce
2 teaspoons sugar
¼ teaspoon ground white pepper
1 spring onion, coarsely chopped

Halve the peppers, removing seeds and membranes, and slice into strips about 1 inch wide. Heat oil and deep fry the peppers for 2–3 seconds, then add the pork and continue deep frying for another 5 seconds. Remove, drain and set aside.

Pour out all but 1 teaspoon of oil. Stir fry the chili paste for a few seconds, then add fried peppers, pork and all other ingredients. Stir fry for 30 seconds and serve immediately.

JIANG CONG CHAO ZHU GAN & DONG PO ZHOU ZI

Stir-fried Pork Liver & Braised Pork Leg

STIR-FRIED PORK LIVER ⏱

10 ounces pork liver, thinly sliced
2 tablespoons Chinese rice wine
2 teaspoons oil
2 teaspoons finely chopped garlic
1¼ inches ginger root, finely sliced
1 spring onion, cut in 1¼-inch lengths
½ red chili, deseeded and sliced (optional)
1 teaspoon chicken stock powder
1 teaspoon light soy sauce
½ teaspoon sugar
1 teaspoon cornstarch, blended with water

Opposite:
Braised Pork Leg
(top) and Stir-fried
Pork Liver
(bottom).

Marinate liver with wine for about 5 minutes. Heat oil and fry the garlic for a few seconds, then add drained liver, ginger, spring onion and chili (if using). Stir fry over high heat for a few seconds. Add stock powder, soy sauce and sugar and continue stir frying for 1–2 minutes, until the liver is cooked. Thicken with cornstarch and serve immediately.

BRAISED PORK LEG ⏱⏱

1 pork leg, about 2 pounds
2 tablespoons light soy sauce
Oil for deep frying
12 cups chicken stock (page 36)
2 teaspoons dark soy sauce
2½ inches ginger root, sliced
1 teaspoon ground white pepper

Vegetable Garnish:

1 tablespoon oil
10 pieces baby *bok choy* (*bai cai*), blanched
    in boiling water
½ teaspoon salt
¼ teaspoon ground white pepper
¼ teaspoon sesame oil

Heat a large pan of water and simmer the pork leg for 30 minutes. Drain, pat dry and rub the skin with 1 tablespoon of the light soy sauce. Set aside to dry while heating oil for deep frying in a wok. Put in the pork leg and fry over very high heat, turning to brown it all over. Remove, drain and put pork leg in a large bowl of cold water for 10 minutes. Drain.

Combine stock with remaining tablespoon of light soy sauce, dark soy sauce, ginger and pepper. Add the pork leg and simmer over very low heat for about 2 hours, until the pork leg is so tender it can be cut with a spoon. Remove the bone from the center of the pork and put meat on a plate.

Heat ½ cup of the pork stock and thicken with cornstarch. Pour over the pork.

Prepare the **vegetable garnish** by heating the oil in a wok. Add the drained, blanched cabbage, salt, pepper and sesame oil and stir fry for about 30 seconds. Place cabbage around the pork leg and serve immediately.

HEI JIAO NIU ROU

Beef with Black Pepper

Simple and quick to prepare, this Sichuan dish tastes like a flavor-enhanced version of Western black pepper steak, with Sichuan peppercorns adding a distinctive difference. ⏱

8 ounces beef fillet, trimmed and cut in 1-inch cubes
2 tablespoons Chinese rice wine
1 tablespoon water
$^1/_2$ teaspoon salt
$^1/_4$ teaspoon ground white pepper
Oil for deep frying
1 tablespoon finely chopped garlic
2 teaspoons coarsely crushed black peppercorns
1 teaspoon crushed Sichuan peppercorns or *sansho*
2 teaspoons oyster sauce
2 teaspoons light soy sauce
1 teaspoon sesame oil
Sliced lettuce for garnish

Put beef in a bowl and sprinkle with wine, water, salt and white pepper. Massage well for about 30 seconds until all the liquid is absorbed by the beef.

Heat oil and deep fry the beef over very high heat for 30 seconds. Drain and set aside. Tip out all but 1 teaspoon of oil and stir fry the garlic for a few seconds, then add the beef and all other ingredients, except for the lettuce. Stir fry for a few seconds until well mixed and serve immediately on a bed of shredded lettuce.

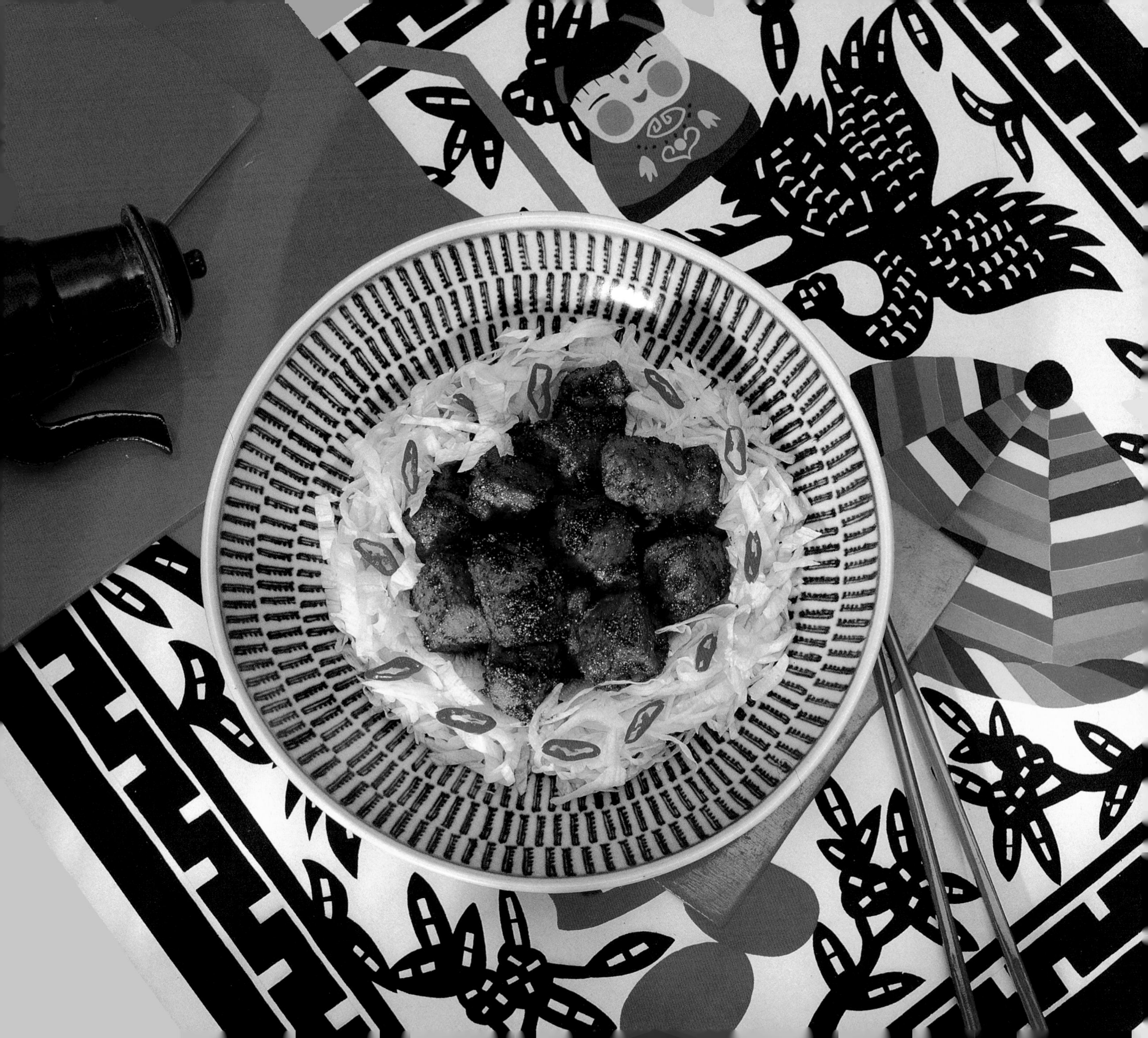

ZHI MA NIU PAI

Deep-fried Beef with Sesame Seeds

An excellent way of preparing beef, with the outside of the meat still crunchy despite the coating of sauce. ⏱

8 ounces beef fillet
$\frac{1}{4}$ teaspoon baking soda
Few drops of liquid meat tenderizer
2 tablespoons water
2 tablespoons cornstarch, blended with water
Oil for deep frying
2 tablespoons lightly toasted sesame seeds

Sauce:

2 teaspoons oil
$1\frac{1}{2}$ teaspoons finely chopped garlic
$1\frac{1}{2}$ teaspoons finely chopped ginger root
1 tablespoon Chinese rice wine
1 teaspoon black soy sauce
1 teaspoon black rice vinegar
2 teaspoons sugar
$\frac{1}{4}$ teaspoon ground white pepper
$\frac{1}{2}$ cup chicken stock (page 36)
2 teaspoons cornstarch, blended with water

Cut the beef into slices $\frac{1}{2}$ inch thick, then place on a chopping board and flatten with the side of a cleaver until $\frac{1}{4}$ inch thick. Put in a bowl and sprinkle with baking soda, meat tenderizer and water. Massage with the hand for 30 seconds, then add blended cornstarch and massage for another 30 seconds. Drain meat and set aside.

Heat oil and deep fry the beef slices for 2–3 minutes until crisp and golden. Drain and set aside.

Make the **sauce** by heating the oil and stir frying garlic and ginger for a few seconds. Add all the sauce ingredients, except cornstarch, and heat through. Thicken with cornstarch, add the beef and mix well to coat the beef with sauce. Serve immediately sprinkled with sesame seeds.

BING TANG YIN ER

White Fungus with Melon Balls

White fungus is believed to be very good for the health, and a warm or chilled sweet soup of fungus and rock sugar is supposed to brighten the eyes as well as refresh the palate. The fungus itself, almost devoid of calories and virtually tasteless, is prized for its texture as well as its health-giving properties. Combined here with melon balls, it makes a delicious light conclusion to any meal. ◑

1½ ounces dried white fungus
3 ounces rock sugar
3 cups water
3 ounces Hami melon, rock melon
    or honeydew

Wash the fungus well, then soak in warm water for 1 hour. Remove the stems and any tough portions and cut into bite-sized pieces. Set aside.

Heat rock sugar and water in a pan, stirring until sugar dissolves. Pour into a bowl and add the white fungus. Cover the bowl and put in a steamer. Steam for 1½ hours until the fungus is soft. Leave to cool, then chill.

Just before serving, make small balls of the melon. Add to the chilled fungus and serve in small individual bowls.

Opposite:
White Fungus with Melon Balls (top right) seen with decorative birds and rabbits made from dough.

LIAN ZI HONG DOU SHA & DOU SHA WO BING

Red Bean Soup & Red Bean Pancakes

Red azuki beans are popular for sweet dishes and cakes, and are often made into a paste which is sold in cans. This red bean soup is generally served as a snack in China, and is particularly popular with children. Red bean paste makes a smooth filling in the well-known Sichuan red bean pancake; in this version, the cook adds a touch of custard powder to the batter, showing that Chinese cooks are not afraid to adopt products from the West.

RED BEAN SOUP ⊘

$1\frac{1}{2}$ ounces dried or canned lotus nuts
8 ounces dried red azuki beans (1 cup)
1 strip dried or fresh orange peel
4 cups water
$\frac{1}{2}$–$\frac{3}{4}$ cup sugar

If using dried lotus nuts, soak in hot water for $1\frac{1}{2}$ hours, drain, peel and use a toothpick to push out the bitter central core. If using canned nuts, drain and discard liquid.

Soak the red beans in warm water to cover for 30 minutes. Drain and combine with orange peel and water and simmer gently, covered, for 1 hour. Add the lotus nuts and cook for 1 more hour. Add sugar to taste and stir until dissolved. Serve warm.

RED BEAN PANCAKES ⊘ ⊘

$1\frac{1}{4}$ cups white flour, sifted
$\frac{1}{4}$ teaspoon custard powder
1 egg
Water to mix
4 ounces red bean paste (see Helpful hints)
Oil for shallow frying

Combine flour, custard powder, egg and sufficient water to make a batter the consistency of thin cream. Heat wok and grease with 1 teaspoon oil, swirling the wok around so that the oil covers all sides. Pour in about $\frac{1}{4}$ cup of the batter and swirl the wok around to make a thin pancake. Cook until the top of the pancake has set and the underside is golden. Remove, set aside and repeat until the batter is used up.

Place the pancakes, browned side up, on a flat surface. Spread the center of each pancake with bean paste and fold in the edges to enclose the paste. Heat a little oil in a wok and fry the stuffed pancake until golden. Cut into bite-sized pieces and serve.

Helpful hints: If canned red bean paste is not available, soak $\frac{1}{2}$ cup red beans for 2 hours. Steam until soft with a strip of dried orange peel. Mash, adding sugar to taste. Red dates may be steamed with the beans for additional flavor, if desired.

MANG GUO BU DING & ZHEN ZHU CI

Mango Pudding & Glutinous Rice Dumplings

MANG GUO BU DING ❷❷

1 medium-sized ripe mango (about 8 ounces)
3 teaspoons powdered gelatin
1 cup hot water
1 cup iced water
½ cup thick or whipping cream, unbeaten
1 cup coconut milk

Peel mango and cut the flesh into tiny dice. Sprinkle the gelatin over hot water and leave to swell for 5 minutes. Stir until completely dissolved, then combine with all other ingredients, including mango. Pour into 6 individual bowls and refrigerate until set. Unmold and serve with additional cream if liked. This Westernized dessert is popular in parts of southern China and Hong Kong.

Opposite:
Mango Pudding
(bottom) and
Glutinous Rice
Dumplings
(top right).

GLUTINOUS RICE DUMPLINGS ❷❷

⅔ cup glutinous rice flour
1 tablespoon white flour
About ¼ cup water
3½ ounces pearl sago, soaked in warm water
     for 5 minutes, drained
3 red cherries, halved

Filling:
½ cup black sesame seeds
Oil for deep frying nuts
1 heaped tablespoon raw peanuts
1 heaped tablespoon walnut pieces
¼ cup lard, very finely chopped
3 tablespoons sugar

Make **filling** first. Dry fry sesame seeds over low heat, stirring, until crisp. Set aside. Heat oil and deep fry the peanuts until cooked. Drain, cool and rub off skins. Cover the walnuts with boiling water and soak for 5 minutes. Rub off the skins and dry the walnuts. Deep fry in oil used for peanuts, then drain. Chop or process the sesame seeds, peanuts, walnuts and lard together until very fine. Mix in sugar and set aside.

Combine glutinous rice flour and white flour and mix with water to make a smooth, pliable dough. Divide into 6 pieces and flatten each into a circle about 2½ inches in diameter. Put one-sixth of the filling, rolled into a ball, in the center of the dough and wrap up, pinching together and shaping with the hands to make a smooth ball. Repeat until you have 6 dumplings.

Put the drained sago on a plate and roll each dumpling to coat with sago. Put dumplings on a plate and steam over high heat for 5 minutes. Remove to a serving plate, decorate each dumpling with a cherry half and serve warm or at room temperature.

BA SI PING GUO

Candied Apples

Apples or crisp Chinese pears can be used for this delightful dessert. It is important that everything be laid out in preparation so that the final stages of cooking can be done rapidly. The photograph opposite uses the tiny apples available in many parts of China during summer months. ⊘⊘

> **4 large green apples, peeled, cored and**
> **cut into 8 slices**
> **Oil for deep frying**

Batter:
> **1 cup white flour**
> **2 tablespoons cornstarch**
> **1 teaspoon baking soda**
> **$\frac{1}{2}$ beaten egg**
> **Water as required**

Syrup:
> **$\frac{1}{2}$ cup sugar**
> **2 tablespoons water**

Prepare the **batter** by combining all ingredients, adding enough water to achieve the consistency of a thick cream.

Heat the sugar and water over moderate heat, stirring, until the **syrup** turns golden brown. Keep warm.

Have a bowl of iced water and a greased serving dish ready. Heat oil for deep frying. When it is very hot, dip slices of apple, a few at a time, into the batter and fry until golden brown. Remove from oil, drain, and dip into the syrup, turning to coat thoroughly. Plunge apple slices immediately into the iced water to set the syrup into a toffee-like coating, then put on the serving dish. Serve immediately.

Mail-order Sources of Ingredients

The ingredients used in this book can all be found in markets featuring the foods of Southeast Asia. Many of them can also be found in any well-stocked supermarket. Ingredients not found locally may be available from the mail-order markets listed below.

Anzen Importers
736 NE Union Ave.
Portland, OR 97232
Tel: 503-233-5111

Central Market
40th & Lamar St.
Austin, TX 78756
Tel: 512-206-1000

Dean & Deluca
560 Broadway
New York, NY 10012
Tel: 800-221-7714 (outside NY)
      800-431-1691 (in NY)

Dekalb World Farmers Market
3000 East Ponce De Leon
Decatur, GA 30034
Tel: 404-377-6401

Gourmail, Inc.
816 Newton Road
Berwyn, PA 19312
Tel: 215-296-4620

House of Spices
76-17 Broadway
Jackson Heights
Queens, NY 11373
Tel: 718-507-4900

Kam Man Food Products
200 Canal Street
New York, NY 10013
Tel: 212-755-3566

Nancy's Specialty Market
P.O. Box 327
Wye Mills, MD 21679
Tel: 800-462-6291

Oriental Food Market and Cooking School
2801 Howard St.
Chicago, IL 60645
Tel: 312-274-2826

Oriental Market
502 Pampas Drive
Austin, TX 78752
Tel: 512-453-9058

Pacific Mercantile Company, Inc.
1925 Lawrence St.
Denver, CO 80202
Tel: 303-295-0293

Penn Herbs
603 North 2nd St.
Philadelphia, PA 19123
Tel: 800-523-9971

Rafal Spice Company
2521 Russell
Detroit, MI 48207
Tel: 313-259-6373

Siam Grocery
2745 Broadway
New York, NY 10025
Tel: 212-245-4660

Spice House
1048 N. Old World 3rd St.
Milwaukee, WI
Tel: 414-272-0977

Thailand Food Corp.
4821 N. Broadway St.
Chicago, IL 60640
Tel: 312-728-1199

Uwajimaya
PO Box 3003
Seattle, WA 98114
Tel: 206-624-6248

Vietnam Imports
922 W. Broad Street
Falls Church, VA 22046
Tel: 703-534-9441

Index